MO
SOCIETY FOR RESEARCH IN
CHILD DEVELOPMENT
Serial No. 229, Vol. 57, No. 5, 1992

TESTIFYING IN CRIMINAL COURT: EMOTIONAL EFFECTS ON CHILD SEXUAL ASSAULT VICTIMS

Gail S. Goodman
Elizabeth Pyle Taub
David P. H. Jones
Patricia England
Linda K. Port
Leslie Rudy
Lydia Prado

WITH COMMENTARIES BY
John E. B. Myers
Gary B. Melton

MONOGRAPHS OF THE SOCIETY FOR RESEARCH IN CHILD DEVELOPMENT
Serial No. 229, Vol. 57, No. 5, 1992

CONTENTS

ABSTRACT

Goodman, Gail S.; Taub, Elizabeth Pyle; Jones, David P. H.; England, Patricia; Port, Linda K.; Rudy, Leslie; and Prado, Lydia. Testifying in Criminal Court: Emotional Effects on Child Sexual Assault Victims. With Commentaries by John E. B. Myers and Gary B. Melton. *Monographs of the Society for Research in Child Development*, 1992, **57**(5, Serial No. 229).

Child victims must cope not only with the emotional consequences of criminal acts but also with the potentially traumatizing effects of legal involvement. Dramatic increases in the reporting of child sexual abuse are bringing greater numbers of children into contact with the criminal justice system, raising fears that child victims of sex crimes will be further harmed by the courts. In the present study, the effects of criminal court testimony on child sexual assault victims were examined in a sample of 218 children. From this sample, the behavioral disturbance of a group of "testifiers" was compared to that of a matched control group of "nontestifiers" at three points following testimony: 3 months, 7 months, and after prosecution ended. At 7 months, testifiers evinced greater behavioral disturbance than nontestifiers, especially if the testifiers took the stand multiple times, were deprived of maternal support, and lacked corroboration of their claims. Once prosecution ended, adverse effects of testifying diminished. In courthouse interviews before and after testifying, the main fear expressed by children concerned having to face the defendant. Children who appeared more frightened of the defendant while testifying were less able to answer the prosecutors' questions; and later, after the cases were closed, they were more likely to say that testifying had affected them adversely. The two most pervasive predictors of children's experiences in the courtroom, however, were age and severity of abuse. Despite relevant laws, few innovative techniques were used to help the children testify. The results are discussed in relation to children's ability to cope with stressful situations, the interaction of the legal system with the child/family system, and debates about the need to protect child victims who testify in criminal court.

I. INTRODUCTION

An upsurge in the reporting of child sexual abuse is bringing an increasing number of children into the criminal justice system, accompanied by the legal and psychological dilemmas that such cases pose. One of these dilemmas concerns how to prosecute without causing additional trauma to children and without abrogating defendants' rights. Despite growing concern, we know surprisingly little about the effects of criminal court testimony on child victims of sexual abuse; the purpose of the present study was to redress this lack.[1]

It is common knowledge that testifying can be a stressful experience even for adult witnesses. Although we know little about children's responses to testifying, studies of children's reactions to other stressful situations (e.g., see Garmezy & Rutter, 1983) may help guide child witness research. Such studies suggest that factors associated with the system of the child (e.g., individual differences, such as age and gender), the family (e.g., maternal support), and the law (e.g., prolonged or repeated exposure to a stressful environment) would all be expected to affect children's emotional reactions to testifying in court.

In the present *Monograph*, we develop this framework in relation to child witnesses. Before doing so, however, it is necessary to examine the extent and characteristics of children's involvement in child sexual abuse prosecutions and review existing research on children's reactions to legal involvement.

CHILDREN AS WITNESSES IN SEXUAL ABUSE CASES

The United States has recently experienced a phenomenal growth in reports of child sexual abuse. When the National Center on Child Abuse

---

[1] Some prefer the term "alleged victim" because in actual cases of child sexual abuse one cannot always distinguish true from false reports with absolute certainty. For the sake of brevity, we have chosen the term "victim." All the children were in the role of victim in the prosecutions.

and Neglect began collecting data in 1976, child protection agencies nation-wide reported 1,975 cases of child sexual assault. By 1990, the total came to 138,357 (Department of Health and Human Services, 1992). Compared to other kinds of abuse and neglect cases, sexual abuse cases more often involve the courts (American Association for Protecting Children, 1988); in fact, by prosecutors' reports, children in America are more likely to testify in such cases than in any other kind of criminal case (Leippe, Brigham, Cousins, & Romanczyk, 1989; Whitcomb, Shapiro, & Stellwagen, 1985).

Although courtroom testimony is not always required, it may play an important part in successful prosecution of child sexual abuse cases because the unique character of this crime heightens the chances that the child's testimony will be needed. It is not uncommon for the assault to leave little sign; once completed, acts of fondling and oral sex—which are more common than rape—are largely invisible. Moreover, when weeks, months, or even years elapse before a child reveals that abuse has occurred, the likelihood that physical evidence of the assault will remain is reduced. Even when such evidence exists, it may have to be linked by the child's testimony to a specific perpetrator. The child's account is thus likely to be a crucial piece of evidence heard by a grand jury or presented at a preliminary hearing and trial.

No yearly statistics are kept concerning the number of child sexual abuse victims who become involved in criminal prosecutions and who testify, but relevant information is available.[2] Such information indicates considerable variability across jurisdictions in the number of child sexual abuse cases prosecuted and the number of children who testify. Concerning the number of cases prosecuted, a 1981 American Bar Association survey of prosecutors across the United States indicated that about 75% of intrafamilial and 80% of extrafamilial sexual abuse cases referred to district attorneys' offices resulted in prosecution; about two-thirds of these were settled by guilty pleas (Bulkley, 1983). However, in a later survey, some jurisdictions claimed that 41% of child sexual assault cases went to trial (Whitcomb et al., 1985). The most recent statistics come from a national telephone survey of 530 district attorneys' offices (Smith, 1991), which uncovered a range of from 1 to 800 ($M = 66$) in the number of child sexual assault cases prosecuted by each office.

Differences across jurisdictions in the incidence of child sexual abuse and in sentiment, state law, and resources concerning its prosecution may

---

[2] It is unfortunate that there are no general statistics on the number of children who are subpoenaed and who testify in various types of criminal court proceedings. Although such data would be helpful, it should be noted that they would vary as a function of the historical and cultural contexts that affect laws influencing prosecution (e.g., corroboration laws), prosecutors' decisions to pursue child sexual abuse cases, the willingness of children and families to report sexual abuse, etc.

at least in part explain these diverging statistics as well as variability in the number of children who testify. Concerning the latter, Rogers (1980) followed 261 child sexual abuse cases reported to police in the District of Columbia and discovered that few children took the stand at trial. In contrast, Sas and Wolfe (1991) substantiated that 50% of the 150 children involved in a study on preparing children for court later testified either at trial or in some type of preliminary hearing. In considering such statistics, it is important to keep in mind that, even in cases settled before trial, children may be required to testify at competence examinations and/or preliminary hearings.

Increased awareness of the extent of child sexual abuse (Finkelhor, 1984; Russell, 1983) and of its emotional sequelae (for reviews, see Browne & Finkelhor, 1986; and Wyatt & Powell, 1988) has brought considerable public and legislative attention to the issue of children's ability to withstand court proceedings. Courtrooms are austere, formal settings capable of intimidating adults, let alone children. The court system, established with adult defendants and witnesses in mind, does not easily accommodate children's special needs. Nevertheless, various groups have made recommendations for changes in current procedures when a child victim testifies (e.g., *Attorney General's Task Force on Family Violence*, 1984; Bulkley, 1982), and legislatures across the country have recently passed new laws governing children's testimony. These new laws promote the use of videotaped testimony and closed-circuit television, the extension of hearsay exceptions, early docketing of cases involving child victims, and the use of expert witnesses to testify about the effects of sexual abuse (for reviews, see Bulkley, 1982; and Goodman, 1984). In addition, courts are being asked to rule on the use of innovative procedures in individual cases (e.g., *Craig v. Maryland*, 1991). The purpose of these reforms is to minimize the presumed traumatic effects on children of court appearances and maximize children's ability to provide accurate testimony. Some of the new laws have been deemed unconstitutional (*Coy v. Iowa*, 1988) because they overly infringe on the Sixth Amendment rights of defendants, especially those of face-to-face confrontation and cross-examination of all witnesses. Other reforms, however, have withstood constitutional test (*Maryland v. Craig*, 1990).

Despite the enthusiasm for procedural reform, systematic research about children's immediate or long-term psychological reactions to court involvement has been scarce, and much of the existing evidence is anecdotal (Benedek, 1982; Berliner & Barbieri, 1984; Claman, Harris, Bernstein, & Lovitt, 1986; Levine & Levine, 1992; Pynoos & Eth, 1984; Schudson, 1987; Terr & Watson, 1980; Weiss & Berg, 1982). Nevertheless, many attorneys, mental health professionals, and legal commentators have claimed that court involvement retraumatizes children (e.g., Bulkley, 1982; Burgess & Holmstrom, 1978; Katz & Mazur, 1979; Libai, 1969; Parker, 1982), while

3

others have asserted that it is not necessarily traumatic and may at times be cathartic (Berliner & Barbieri, 1984; Goodman, Levine, Melton, & Ogden, 1990). We review next what is known from scientific study about children's reactions to testifying.

THE FINDINGS OF PREVIOUS RESEARCH

Only a few published studies have focused on children's psychological reactions to court proceedings. The reason for this paucity is probably two-fold. First, until relatively recent times, it was generally believed that children rarely testify in courts of law, and child sexual abuse itself was not believed to be widespread, a misconception shattered by findings of recent prevalence studies (Finkelhor, 1984; Russell, 1983). Second, the criminal justice system poses many formidable obstacles for the researcher. Among the few who braved it, the earliest were Gibbens and Prince (1963). Working through records of the Federation of Committees for the Moral Welfare of Children in England, they compared the adjustment of a selected sample of child victims who were involved in court proceedings with that of a random sample of those who did not go to court. They found that 56% of the no-court group evinced no overt signs of disturbance and seemed to recover quickly whereas only 18% of the court group did. However, they also noted that the cases ending in court were probably the more serious and that the families of the court group were more disturbed; thus, the greater disturbance evinced by the children who appeared in court might have resulted from factors other than involvement in court proceedings.

DeFrancis (1969) followed 250 cases of child sexual assault and incest in New York, of which 173 resulted in prosecution. He reported that numerous court appearances were required of the children and that their testimony resulted in "much stress and tension" for them and in resentment in their parents. However, because no comparison group was included, it is impossible to tell how much of the children's disturbance may have been caused by the assault rather than by their legal involvement; moreover, no standardized measures of the children's and families' psychological adjustment were used. Nevertheless, this study transmits the impression that legal involvement was stressful for children and their families.

Nearly 20 years elapsed before the next study was published. Tedesco and Schnell (1987) sent a questionnaire concerning legal experiences to 120 child abuse councils, mental health facilities, therapists, and others who provide services to child victims in Iowa, asking that they be distributed to children who had testified in criminal court; 48 of these were returned, completed either by the victims, sometimes with the help of a parent ($N = 35$), or by an adult (attorney, social worker, or relative other than a parent).

The victims ranged in age from 4 to 22 years, and 81% were females; only nine (all females) had actually testified in court. Of those nine, only two (22%) found the legal process helpful, whereas, of the 31 who did not testify, 21 (68%) rated it as such. Among all respondents, the number of interviews endured was negatively correlated with perceived helpfulness. Females and incest victims appeared to be more conflicted than males and nonincest victims, the former being more likely to rate the legal process as both helpful and harmful; interestingly, treatment workers were more likely to rate the procedures as harmful than were parents or child victims. Although intriguing, these findings are difficult to assess for a variety of reasons, including the low return rate (40%), the likely unrepresentativeness of the resulting sample, and the lack of statistical control over potentially correlated variables (e.g., sex and type of charge, abuse severity and courtroom testimony). The impression that emerges, however, is that courtroom testimony and numerous precourt interviews of children contribute to feelings that the legal process is not helpful.

At the same time as Tedesco and Schnell's study appeared, Oates and Tong (1987) reported a retrospective study in which 229 child sexual abuse cases in Australia were traced 2.6 years after the victims had been referred to a hospital for evaluation. Although only 49 families agreed to participate in the study, these were representative of the larger sample in terms of the children's age, gender, and relationship to the defendant and the families' socioeconomic status. Forty-six of the parents completed a structured interview. For these families, 21 of the cases went to court, 12 heard in children's and 9 in criminal court. Children were required to testify in only 6 of the 21 court hearings, all of which involved criminal prosecutions. Using a five-point scale ("not upset at all" to "extremely upset"), 18 of the 21 nonoffending parents indicated that their children had been very upset immediately after the court hearings, and 12 reported that, even 2.6 years later, their children were still upset about their court experience. In addition, compared to the others, children whose cases went to court were more likely to be reported by their parents as having behavioral problems at school. Although this interesting study suffers from many of the methodological problems mentioned above, it indicates that court involvement is stressful for children.

The most impressive study to date was conducted in North Carolina by Runyan, Everson, Edelsohn, Hunter, and Coulter (1988); although their research mainly concerned children's reactions to juvenile court experience, it included a small sample of children who were also involved in criminal court proceedings. The full group comprised 75 sexual abuse victims, aged 6–17 years, whose cases involved a family member or caretaker as the alleged perpetrator. The children's well-being was assessed by, among other measures, a psychiatric interview conducted early in the social service and legal intervention process and repeated 5 months later. By the second interview, 12 children had testified in juvenile court; these twelve proved to have had higher initial distress scores than the 63 children who had not testified. When initial differences in relationship to the perpetrator, vaginal penetration, verbal IQ, percentage of life having been abused, and provision of therapy were statistically controlled, children who testified in juvenile court exhibited significant improvement in their anxiety scores compared with the others.

Of primary interest for our own research were the 22 children for whom criminal proceedings were pending. Across the 5-month period, they were only 8% as likely to evince improvement (i.e., to show a 1 standard deviation or more decrease in their depression score) on the depression subscale as the 33 children not involved in the court process. Thus, over the course of the 5 months, children not involved in criminal proceedings showed significantly greater improvement, leading Runyan et al. to conclude that waiting for criminal prosecution has a negative effect on children whereas testifying in juvenile court has a beneficial effect.

Although this study improves in many ways on former research, it too has its limitations. Of primary concern is that the children who testified in juvenile court were more disturbed at the *initial* interview than those who did not testify; at the 5-month follow-up, the two groups actually looked very similar. Thus, the "improvement" of the children who had testified in juvenile court may simply represent either unaided recovery or regression to the mean, and it may in fact say little about any beneficial effects of testifying.

A second concern is that the comparison between children who testified in juvenile court and those who were awaiting criminal proceedings is confounded by the fact that proceedings were completed for the former but still in progress for the latter. It is possible that closure would lead to improvement whatever the type of case. Finally, because only five children in the entire study testified in criminal court, the effect of criminal court testimony could not be ascertained.

Despite these problems, Runyan et al.'s study shows that testifying in juvenile court did not cause the children additional harm: the children's scores tended to improve over time regardless of court experience. If this finding were to be replicated for testimony in criminal court, it would argue against the notion that legal involvement traumatizes children.

In summary, the few existing studies generally indicate that criminal court involvement is stressful for children, especially if in-court testimony and repeated interviewing are required. Although such involvement may not lead to disturbance greater than what is evinced at entry into the legal system, it may keep children from improving at the same rate as they would if they were not involved in criminal court. However, owing to a variety of methodological problems, it is difficult to take these conclusions as firmly established.

Nevertheless, there are a number of reasons to suspect that these general conclusions would be supported by more ideal studies. Legal involvement can be stressful even for adult victims of sex crimes (Brownmiller, 1975; Katz & Mazur, 1979); however, adults' more complete emotional development may help bolster them compared to children against short- and long-term adverse effects of stressful events (Maccoby, 1983). Moreover, the potential for legal-system-induced stress in children is exacerbated by a number of factors.

First, in contrast to adult victims, children, especially in intrafamilial cases, are likely to be interviewed before a court appearance by social service workers as well as police and attorneys; additional precourt interviews may be required if children's disclosures are not readily forthcoming or because they simply tend to report less information than adults (e.g., Goodman & Reed, 1986; Leippe, Romanczyk, & Manion, 1991; Marin, Holmes, Guth, & Kovac, 1979). Then, young children may have to make more court appearances than adults as, for example, when a competence examination is required. Thus, child victims are likely to endure an even greater number of interviews than adult victims. Second, it is not uncommon for children to be subjected to months, if not years, of uncertainty about whether their courtroom testimony will be needed. Young children's inability to gauge passage of time as accurately as older children or adults may add to their sense of unpredictability about legal involvement (e.g., Friedman, 1982). As often occurs in other stressful situations, lack of predictability might exacerbate distress (e.g., Ross & Ross, 1988). Third, compared to adults, children have a poor understanding of the legal system (Cashmore & Bussey, 1990; Melton, 1989; Pierre-Puysegur, 1985; Saywitz, 1989; Warren-Leubecker, Tate, Hinton, & Ozbek, 1989). They might not understand why they have to go to court, what will happen there, whether they are to blame, and why their testimony might be challenged. Fourth, the child's relationship to the defendant is also likely to add to the stress. Strangers are relatively infrequently implicated as perpetrators of child sex crimes; children are much more likely to accuse an adult known to them, such as a relative, the mother's boyfriend, a teacher, or a neighbor (Finkelhor, 1984). In many such cases, the child's emotional tie to the accused increases the stress and guilt that accompany testifying. Although perpetrators in adult rape cases are also often known to the victim, the feeling of dependence on, and intimidation by, the perpetrator may be even greater for many child than adult victims. Finally, regardless of age, courtroom testimony is likely to force the victim to relive the assault and to do so in public. Given the aura of both intimacy and taboo that surrounds most sexual activity, having to describe such acts publicly is likely to be embarrassing and humiliating. For all these reasons, child victims may find courtroom testimony traumatizing as well as retraumatizing.

Alternatively, there are some reasons to believe that testifying may be cathartic or empowering for children. Victimization is likely to weaken a child's sense of control, and testimony potentially places her in a more powerful role, where she can influence the outcome of a case (Berliner & Barbieri, 1984). Moreover, being called to testify represents public acknowledgment that the child's claim is taken seriously. And, especially if her testimony leads to a guilty verdict, the child may feel that her statements mattered and that justice was done. If not permitted to testify, the child might feel disenfranchised. It is also possible that, compared to adults, children may be treated with greater consideration by defense attorneys, who might fear that jurors will sympathize with the child victim if she is harshly questioned and who might themselves be truly concerned with the child's well-being. Judges, too, may go out of their way to protect child victims.

Systematic research can help resolve debates about beneficial versus harmful effects of testifying on children. It would seem likely that who is helped and who harmed depends on specifiable conditions revolving around child-, family-, and legal-system factors.

COPING WITH STRESSFUL EVENTS: INFLUENCES OF THE CHILD, FAMILY, AND LEGAL SYSTEMS

Although relatively little is known from scientific study about the emotional effects on children of criminal court testimony, studies of children's reactions to other stressful events may provide important insights. Developmental studies of risk factors for psychological disturbance have examined children's reactions to such stressors as parental discord, maternal deprivation, divorce, war, hospitalization, and death of a loved one (for a review, see Rutter, 1983). From these studies, "vulnerability" factors, which increase the effect of stressors, and "protective" factors, which reduce the effect of stressors, have been identified. To the extent that vulnerability and protective factors transcend a specific stressful situation, the factors identified in previous research may also be relevant to child sexual abuse victims' experiences within the legal system. For present purposes, protective and vulnerability factors can be considered within the context of the system of the child, the family, and the law; factors within each system would be expected to influence children's emotional responses to testifying in court.

The child system.—Children's reactions to stressful events differ. The reasons for these differences are only partially understood. However, it is clear that age is one important consideration. The relation between age and emotional distress seems to vary with different stressors. In response to certain stressors (e.g., death of a loved one), younger children have more limited adverse short-term responses (Bowlby, 1980); however, it is possible that adverse long-term reactions may be even greater for younger than for older children (Rutter, 1983). In response to other stressors (e.g., hospitalization), the adverse short- and long-term effects are stronger for younger than older children, especially if the stressor affects a developing socioemotional system (e.g., parental attachment) and the child's ability to understand the event is limited (Ferguson, 1979; Rutter, 1983). However, for yet other stressful events, it is the form more than the extent of the reaction that is most notable developmentally. In summarizing research on children's reactions to divorce, Rutter (1983) concludes that the form of a child's response (e.g., the specific aspects of the family disruption to which the child responds) is influenced by age but that overall vulnerability is not markedly increased or decreased in any specific age period. Alternatively, Hetherington et al. (1992) report that adverse reactions to divorce and remarriage show less attenuation when adolescents, compared to younger children, are studied.

No previous studies have examined reactions to criminal court involvement as a function of age or developmental level. Studies of children's reactions to other stressful events, as described above, indicate several possible developmental relations. Young children might not realize the significance of legal proceedings, whereas older children might appreciate the importance of their performance, the social implications of public admission of sexual behavior, and the consequences of a guilty or not guilty verdict. This appreciation may add to children's distress. Therefore, younger children may be less adversely affected than children who are older and more aware. Alternatively, younger children may be more easily intimidated and confused by the proceedings given their lack of understanding of the legal system (Cashmore & Bussey, 1990; Pierre-Puysegur, 1985; Saywitz, 1989; Warren-Leubecker et al., 1989) and their general cognitive and emotional immaturity. Older children would be more likely to know what to expect. If so, younger children might be more adversely affected than older children. To investigate these possible relations, it was of interest to include age as a factor in our study.

However, even within an age group, how a child reacts to a stressful event can differ depending on other factors associated with the system of the child, such as the attributions the child makes (e.g., self-blame for the abuse, that the legal system is basically fair), coping mechanisms available to the child (e.g., not looking at the defendant when testifying), the general emotional well-being of the child (e.g., pretestimony level of adjustment, emotional aftermath of the assault), and the child's self-esteem (e.g., that the child basically thinks of himself as a worthwhile person) (Rutter, 1983). In summary, the personal characteristics that a child brings to the courtroom may increase or decrease the likelihood of a maladaptive outcome.

The family system.—In addition to factors associated with the child, factors associated with the child's family system may also play a crucial role. Many stressors, such as sexual abuse and subsequent legal involvement, occur in the context of other, more chronic family problems. Moreover, they can result in family-system changes (e.g., the parents' divorce) that go beyond the original source of distress. In general, persistent disturbance as a result of childhood stressors is more likely if the child comes from a deprived or disturbed family and if the parent-child relationship was poor to start with (Douglas, 1975; Rutter, 1983).

With regard to child sexual abuse specifically, one would suspect that intrafamilial as opposed to extrafamilial child sexual abuse is particularly likely to occur when the family system is characterized by instability and discord and, vice versa, that such abuse would be especially likely to cause increased family turmoil. Thus, children in intrafamilial (e.g., incest) cases might be particularly vulnerable to retraumatization by legal involvement. In addition, the closer the relation of the perpetrator to the child (e.g., the perpetrator is a father or stepfather), the more distressed the child might be by legal involvement (e.g., due to guilt, family pressure not to disclose). Thus, testifying against a loved one might well be associated with greater strain for children.

The literature on children's reactions to stressful events suggests that, in general, parental support and parental rejection are, respectively, protective (Elder, 1979; Rutter, 1971) and vulnerability (Rohner & Rohner, 1980) factors. Although supportive relationships with persons other than the parents can also serve a protective function (Garmezy, 1983), many children can be expected to look primarily to their parents for emotional support.

Consistent with such findings, studies of the emotional effects of sexual abuse on children indicate that maternal support is a particularly important protective factor (e.g., Conte & Berliner, 1988; Conte & Schuerman, 1987). However, level of maternal support provided to children in intrafamilial sexual abuse cases is related to the mother's relationship to the offender: Everson, Hunter, Runyon, Edelsohn, and Coulter (1989) found that mothers were more supportive of their children if the offender was an ex-spouse than if the offender was someone with whom the mother still maintained a relationship. In any case, to the extent that maternal support is a protective factor across many stressful situations, it may be an important family-system factor for children who testify in sexual abuse cases.

The legal system.—Research on children's reactions to stressful situations points to certain experiences within the legal system itself as likely to be associated with adverse or beneficial reactions. For example, prolonged exposure to a stressor can be detrimental to children's well-being (Garmezy & Rutter, 1983). There is already reason to believe that this relation holds in regard to children's reactions to legal involvement: as described earlier, Runyan et al. (1988) found that more prolonged exposure to the criminal justice system was associated with less improvement in children.

Also of interest, repeated exposure to a stressor can have detrimental effects. In studying children's reactions to hospitalization, researchers find that one hospital admission is not associated with later psychiatric disorder but that having two admissions is associated with a marked increase in risk of subsequent disturbance (Douglas, 1975; Quinton & Rutter, 1976). This effect still holds after family adversity is taken into account. According to Rutter (1983), although the first admission does not lead to disorder, it may predispose the child to react badly the second time. Even one hospital admission has adverse short-term effects, however. Similarly, it is possible that, while stressful for many children, one experience testifying is not in itself detrimental in the long term but that two or more experiences testifying are. As Rutter (1983) concludes, "It could be that single fear-provoking events are of very limited consequence but that many experienced over a short period of time are more likely to be damaging" (p. 15).

In stressful situations, part of children's distress may result from separation from supportive adults while at the same time being exposed to a strange, frightening environment. For example, studies of children's reactions to hospitalization indicate that the stress of hospital visits is reduced by the presence of a familiar figure such as a parent or a consistently present, supportive nurse (Rutter, 1983). It follows that the presence of a parent or other support figure in the courtroom may be a protective factor for children. However, to maintain perceptions of fairness, the legal system often demands that witnesses testify outside the presence of other witnesses. In child sexual abuse cases, parents may also be asked to testify, which typically precludes their presence in the courtroom while the child takes the stand, especially at trial. Because of children's needs for a support person, victim advocates are increasingly assigned to accompany children into the courtroom. However, the benefits of parents or victim advocates as providers of social support for children who testify in court have not been evaluated.

The legal system also typically demands that children, like other witnesses, testify face to face with the defendant, as specified in the Sixth Amendment. Several recent reforms (e.g., use of closed-circuit television or videotaped testimony) revolve around eliminating or modifying the need for children to face the defendant in court, under the assumption that face-to-face confrontation is stressful for child witnesses and inhibits their ability to testify accurately and completely. If this assumption is valid, it would thus be expected that children who are particularly afraid of the defendant would be at greater risk of adverse effects of testifying than children who are less fearful of the defendant.

Summary.—In conclusion, insights into children's reactions to courtroom testimony may be gained from consideration of their reactions to other stressful events. The system of the child, the family, and the law may all contribute to the child's reaction.

CHILDREN'S COURTROOM PERFORMANCE

Although laboratory research on the accuracy and completeness of children's testimony is being actively pursued (see, e.g., Dent & Flin, 1992; and Goodman & Bottoms, in press), researchers have not yet systematically documented children's actual performance as witnesses in criminal court. Similarly, although laboratory studies of mock jurors' perceptions of child witnesses are being conducted, researchers have generally failed to examine the credibility of children who actually testify in court (but see Bottoms & Goodman, 1989).

In laboratory studies, researchers typically find that young children have greater difficulty recalling events and answering questions about their experiences than older children or adults (e.g., Cohen & Harnick, 1980; Goodman, Aman, & Hirschman, 1987; Goodman & Reed, 1986; Leippe et al., 1991; Marin et al., 1979; Nelson, 1986; for reviews, see Kail, 1989; and Spencer & Flin, 1990). Such studies also indicate that testifying face to face in front of a defendant can be intimidating, especially to young children, and result in more limited testimony (e.g., Bussey, Lee, & Ross, 1991; Dent, 1977; Hill & Hill, 1987). Nevertheless, mock jury studies show that young children are viewed as more credible victim/witnesses in sexual assault cases than are older children and adults (Duggan et al., 1989; Goodman, Bottoms, Herscovici, & Shaver, 1989). In addition, surveys of prosecutors indicate that children are viewed as particularly credible witnesses if they show emotion, for example, if they cry while on the stand (Limber & Etheredge, 1989). It is still unknown, however, whether actual child witnesses and jurors exhibit these tendencies.

GOALS AND HYPOTHESES OF THE PRESENT STUDY

Evaluation of the opposing possibilities that testimony may be either traumatic or cathartic in part motivated the present study, as did the search for vulnerability and protective factors. A central goal was to determine if variability in the child and family systems, and in the children's specific experiences within the legal system, would lead to subgroups of children who would be benefited, harmed, or relatively unscathed by testifying.

Although our main focus was on the emotional effects of testifying, we also undertook the task of describing the children's performance and experiences while they testified. Because we were permitted to observe the children testifying in court, we could examine the generalizability of laboratory findings to actual cases; we could also examine the attorneys' and judges' behavior to determine whether the children received harsh treatment or, conversely, protection.

In the process of pursuing these questions, we examined a number of additional issues, such as children's attitudes about going to court (e.g., their specific fears about testifying), use of innovative courtroom techniques to protect children (e.g., testimony via closed-circuit television), and children's and parents' reactions to legal involvement (e.g., their perceptions of the legal system's fairness) once the final disposition of a case was reached. Given the relatively unique opportunity to conduct a large-scale study of child victims' reactions to legal involvement, another goal was to obtain the most complete picture possible.

On the basis of previous research concerning the effects of courtroom testimony and stressful events on children as well as of developmental studies of children's memory and testimony, we formulated a set of hypotheses. These hypotheses and their rationales are presented below.

Our overarching framework emphasizes the interaction of the legal system with the system of the child, along with his or her family. According to this view, a child's experiences in court are partly determined by a unique set of characteristics and resources associated with the child and the child's family and also by how the court responds to those characteristics and resources. Thus, while testifying may be stressful in the short term for many child (as well as adult) witnesses, one might expect that certain subgroups of children would be more at risk of adverse long-term effects of court involvement, depending on how the system treats the child. According to this view, the legal system may have positive or negative emotional effects on children depending on how this interaction is negotiated. It was thus predicted that, on average, children who testify in court proceedings will show greater short-term psychological disturbance than those who do not but that the degree to which the disturbance persists will be a function of interactions among factors associated with the legal system, the family system, and the child system.

The literature reviewed above pointed to several particularly important factors within each system. For the system of the child, the child's age was expected to bear an important influence on his reaction. To the extent that a limited understanding of a stressful or unfamiliar event contributes to adverse emotional effects, younger children's adjustment was predicted to be more negatively affected than older children's. However, to the extent that a better understanding of a stressful event permits a child to worry more about the event and to understand the implications of the event's outcome, older children would be predicted to show greater disturbance than younger children.

The severity of the abuse that the child experienced and the child's fearfulness of the defendant were also predicted to be child-system factors influencing a child's reaction. Testifying in court face to face with the defendant might force the child to reexperience the original trauma, a reliving that would likely be more traumatic if the abuse was severe. Also, fear of the defendant was expected to add to the stress that children might experience anyway by being placed in an austere, foreign environment and publicly questioned about sexual activities.

Within the system of the family, maternal support was expected to be a particularly important protective factor, as it is for children's reactions to sexual abuse generally (e.g., Conte & Schuerman, 1987). Testifying against a parent (e.g., a father or stepfather) was predicted to exacerbate the child's distress; this prediction was based on the notion that testifying against a parent is particularly likely to lead to feelings of conflict and guilt in the child and to be more disruptive of the family system.

Several hypotheses were generated concerning factors involved within the legal system. Specifically, we predicted that children who testify repeatedly, or who experience a greater number of delays and postponements of court hearings, will evince relatively greater disturbance than those who do not. This hypothesis is based on the assumption that prolonged involvement in the criminal justice system and repeated exposure to stressful events are harmful for children (Runyan et al., 1988; Rutter, 1983). Postponements require children to prepare for court without then testifying, which prolongs their involvement and could sensitize them, thereby increasing their anxiety. Testifying many times also prolongs children's involvement and places them in stressful situations repeatedly.

In addition, past research on the accuracy of children's eyewitness testimony led to a set of predictions. Again, these predictions can be considered within the context of the child, family, and legal systems. Specifically, regarding the system of the child, it was predicted that children's ability to testify in court (e.g., to answer questions in detail) would increase with age whereas their perceived credibility would decrease with age, predictions based on findings from relevant laboratory studies (e.g., Goodman & Reed, 1986; Goodman et al., 1989; Leippe et al., 1991). It was also predicted that having to testify about a more severe assault would produce a more emotional reaction, with the result that the quality of the child's testimony (e.g., amount of detail provided) might be adversely affected; nevertheless, children who express distress on the stand (e.g., crying) were expected to be viewed as more credible witnesses (Limber & Etheredge, 1989). Again on the basis of laboratory studies (e.g., Bussey et al., 1991; Dent, 1977), it was predicted that fear of the defendant would impair the amount of detail that children could provide.

Regarding the system of the family, we expected that, owing to feelings of guilt or conflict, children would provide less detail and be more negative about testifying when taking the stand against a parent or stepparent than against an acquaintance or a stranger. Finally, regarding the legal system, it was predicted that, compared to children questioned under standard adversarial conditions, children provided with a more supportive environment (e.g., permitted to take a toy to the stand, permitted to have a parent or victim advocate remain in the courtroom) would evince less fearfulness and provide greater detail about what occurred.

II. DESIGN AND STUDY POPULATION

OVERVIEW

Over 2 years were spent following a group of 218 children through criminal court and collecting data about their experiences. Since our main concern was to determine the emotional effects of testifying on child sexual assault victims, we concentrated most of our attention on the subgroup who took the stand ("testifiers") and a matched subgroup who did not ("controls"). The overall design of the study is presented in Table 1.

In brief, measures of the children's well-being were obtained as soon as possible once the case was referred for prosecution. (The measures are described in detail in the subsequent chapter on measures.) This assessment consisted of the children's primary caretakers completing the Child Behavior Checklist (CBCL) and the children's teachers completing the Teacher Report Form (TRF), both of which provide T scores for the children's total behavior problems, internalizing problems, and externalizing problems. This assessment permitted us to determine children's level of adjustment before extensive legal involvement and courtroom testimony had occurred. We also began to document the case through an adaptation of the Sexual Assault Profile (SAP), on which we rated the severity of the abuse, the child's relation to the defendant, etc. When the children were later subpoenaed, we met them at the courthouse to obtain additional measures of their well-being and to interview them about their upcoming court appearance; we then waited with them to see whether they would be called to the stand. Children who did testify were observed as they underwent direct and cross-examination (noting their responses and the nature of the questioning) and then reinterviewed immediately after they were excused from the courtroom. To test our hypotheses about the effects of courtroom testimony, measures of the control and testifying children's well-being were obtained 3 and 7 months after the latter group first testified and again after the case was closed. We could thus determine at each follow-up whether the children who testified showed greater emotional disturbance than their matched con-

TABLE 1

Experimental Design and Measures Used in the Study

Intake (N = 218; home visit, after subpoena issued):
  Informed consent (parent and child)
  Sexual Assault Profile (SAP; DA's files, primary caretaker and child report)
  Achenbach Child Behavior Checklist (CBCL; primary caretaker report)
  Social Adjustment Scale (SAS; primary caretaker self-report)
Precourt (N = 110; court offices; unknown whether child will testify):
  Spielberger State Anxiety Scale
  Before-Court Measure (child's feelings about having to testify in court)
  Abbreviated form of the CBCL (by parent; child distress in last 48 hours)
Court—testifiers only (N = 40 at preliminary hearings; N = 8 at competence
    examinations; and N = 17 at trial):
  Court observations (ratings of child and of court members)
Postcourt—testifiers only (N = 38):
  After-Court Measure (court offices, child's feelings about the experience)
Follow-up, 3 months (N: testifiers = 46; controls = 46; matched pairs = 46):
  Achenbach Child Behavior Checklist
Follow-up, 7 months (N: testifiers = 37; controls = 37; matched pairs = 37):
  Achenbach Child Behavior Checklist
Follow-up, final (N: testifiers = 28; controls = 28; matched pairs = 28):
  Achenbach Child Behavior Checklist
  Case progress (facts concerning progress through the legal system; obtained also
    from additional nontestifier group, N = 218)
  Legal Involvement Questionnaire (parent's and child's reactions to experiences in
    the legal system; obtained also from additional nontestifier group, N = 73
    children and 103 caretakers; of these, N = 57 children and 85 caretakers
    for closed cases)

Note.—The total sample (N = 218) comprises testifiers, matched controls, and additional nontestifiers.

trols. Finally, we surveyed the families to obtain the children's and parents' attitudes toward the legal system.

VICTIMS, DEFENDANTS, AND CASE CHARACTERISTICS

Intake Procedures

Between September 1985 and December 1987, we worked with three district attorneys' (DAs') offices in the Denver area to obtain our sample. DAs' offices were used as the referral source for several reasons. First, cases referred for prosecution are likely to contain a higher percentage of certifiable crimes than are cases reported to the police or social services; this, in effect, provided us with an initial screening for possible false reports. Second, parents wisely wanted to be assured that our study would not interfere with prosecution of the case. By working through the DAs' offices and making certain that the DAs approved of our measures and procedures, such assurance could be provided.

There were a number of other advantages as well. Access to the prosecutors' files allowed us to obtain information about a case without extensive questioning of the victim and family about the assault. The DAs' cooperation was also beneficial in convincing judges to let us remain in the courtroom even when it was closed to others. As concerns the ethics of soliciting participants for the study, we could not call families directly because their names were not a matter of public information. Instead, as they would normally do, victim advocates (VAs) in the DAs' offices called the family to inform them of the expected course of legal events when a child sexual assault case was filed for prosecution. At that time, the VAs also mentioned our study and asked if the family wanted to be contacted for further information; if the family granted permission, we contacted them, explained the study, and scheduled an appointment. If the family did not have a phone, they were contacted through the mail by the VAs and then by us.

Total Sample

Victims.—During the period when we solicited participants, 359 cases were referred for prosecution. Owing mainly to refusals or inability to maintain contact with a family (e.g., the family moved) but also to unexpected complications (e.g., one child whose case was filed in the wrong jurisdiction), the final sample consisted of 218 children; characteristics of the sample are presented in Table 2. As can be seen in that table, the children ranged widely in age. When the abuse was first reported to authorities, over 55% were under 10 years of age, and 18% were 5 years old or younger; as far as could be ascertained, for some of the children the assault began when they were as young as 2 years. The majority of victims were girls and Anglo. Although the socioeconomic (SES) level of the families (assessed through a revision of the Hollingshead scale; Watt, 1976) varied across the entire seven-point range, middle to lower socioeconomic status was typical ($M = 4.94$; SD = 1.57).

Defendants.—Because our study involved criminal and not juvenile court, the defendants' ages did not drop below 18 years. Nearly all were male; two of the six female defendants were charged with committing criminal acts in conjunction with males. Many at least initially denied the charges, although a substantial minority admitted that some part of the acts occurred. Note that an admission is not the same as a confession—it may be a minimalization of the abuse in light of the child's report or the medical evidence, or it may consist of acknowledging that certain acts occurred but justifying them in the context of nonabusive activities (e.g., washing the child's genitals).

Nearly all the defendants were known to the children. The largest categories of offenders were natural fathers (15%), stepfathers (9%), live-in boyfriends (11%), family friends (14%), acquaintances (13%), and neighbors (10%). Forty percent of the defendants were living in the same home with the child when the assault allegedly occurred.

Case characteristics.—Most of the cases involved rape or other forms of genital contact. The abuse lasted anywhere from 1 day to over 5 years, with 75% of the assaults lasting 6 months or less. Only 16% of the children incurred injury as a result of the abuse. Physical force was not always involved, although some of the children had been threatened with guns or knives, and verbal threats were common (e.g., ranging from "You'll get in trouble" or "I'll kill you and your mother if you tell"). Corroborating evidence (e.g., medical evidence, an eyewitness) was available in 34% of the cases.

Most of the children disclosed the abuse relatively quickly (e.g., within 2 weeks), although it took over 6 months for 15% of the children to disclose. The persons to whom the children disclosed the abuse behaved similarly in informing authorities of the abuse; most did so within 2 weeks, but it took 16% over 6 months to do so.

The legal process.—Once the abuse was disclosed to authorities, a police or social service report was taken. Concurrent "dependency and neglect" cases were almost always initiated when intrafamilial abuse was involved and sometimes also if it was not (e.g., cases involving a mother's boyfriend). Within the three jurisdictions that we studied, children rarely testified in dependency and neglect cases (we know of only two instances in our sample).

Once the police or social service report was available, the case was referred to the relevant prosecutor's office. It was at this point that we defined the legal process, by which we mean the prosecution, as beginning. For the 169 cases that reached final disposition (i.e., "closed") during the course of the study, it is possible to provide a sense of the time course of the legal events.

For these cases, the legal process lasted between 2 and 27 months ($M = 10.50$). The time lapse between disclosure of abuse to authorities and holding the first preliminary hearing averaged 4.65 months (range, 0.75–22.75); in 110 of these 169 cases, preliminary hearings were waived. In 51 cases the defendant was bound over for trial, and in 8 cases the charges were dismissed at this point either by the courts or by the DA. The average time lapse between the preliminary hearing and the trial was 4.40 months (range, <1–16.75) and that between the plea bargain or trial and sentencing was 2.0 months. Some defendants were sentenced immediately, but others were not sentenced until over 9 months had passed.

During the course of the children's involvement in the prosecution,

TABLE 2

CHARACTERISTICS OF VICTIMS, DEFENDANTS, AND CASES

A. VICTIMS (168 Girls, 50 Boys, Total $N = 218$)

| | AGE IN YEARS AT: | | | |
	Intake	Report to Authorities	Start of Abuse	End of Abuse
Total:				
Mean	10.05	9.30	8.60	9.00
(Range). . . .	(4–17)	(3–17)	(2–16)	(3–16)
Testifiers:				
Mean	10.22	9.55	8.66	9.29
(Range). . . .	(4–16)	(3–16)	(3–15)	(3–15)
Controls:				
Mean	10.48	9.73	9.03	9.45
(Range). . . .	(4–16)	(3–17)	(2–16)	(3–16)

| | ETHNICITY (%) | | | |
	Anglo	Black	Hispanic	Other
Total	70	11	17	1
Testifiers	75	9	13	2
Controls	80	13	5	1

B. DEFENDANTS (172 Males, 6 Females, Total $N = 178$)

| | ETHNICITY (%) | | | | |
	Anglo	Black	Hispanic	Other	Don't Know
Total	57	16	25	1	2
Testifiers	49	13	31	2	5
Controls	69	16	13	2	0

| | AGE IN YEARS | |
	Mean	Range
Total	35.49	18–78
Testifiers	34.42	19–62
Controls	34.76	18–78

| | INITIAL STANCE (%) | | |
	Denial	Admission	Unknown
Total	42	25	33
Testifiers	64	2	33
Controls	32	32	35

C. CASE CHARACTERISTICS ($N = 218$)

| | RELATIONSHIP TO VICTIM (%) | | | |
	Stranger	Acquaintance/ No Position of Trust	Caregiver/ Position of Trust	Parent/ Stepparent
Total	6	27	43	23
Testifiers.	6	36	42	16
Controls	7	23	45	25

TABLE 2 (*Continued*)

	SEVERITY OF ABUSE		
	Mean	SD	Range
Total	7.88	1.72	4–13

	DURATION OF ABUSE (%)			
	1 Day	2 Days– 6 Months	> 6 Months– 5 Years	> 5 Years
Total	44	31	22	3
Testifiers	51	31	13	6
Controls.....	36	32	31	1

	TYPE OF ABUSE (%)			
	Exhibitionism	Nongenital Fondling	Genital Fondling or Oral Sex	Vaginal or Anal Penetration
Total	1	9	48	42
Testifiers	0	11	47	42
Controls.....	3	7	51	40

	FREQUENCY OF ABUSE (%)			
	1 Time	Limited (2–3 times)	Extended	Unknown
Total	42	21	33	4
Testifiers	51	22	24	4
Control	33	27	33	7

	CHILD INJURED (%)			
	No	Mildly	Moderately	Severely
Total	84	13	3	0
Testifiers	75	20	6	0
Control	93	4	3	0

	FORCE INVOLVED (%)			
	No	Mild	Moderate	Severe
Total	62	23	16	3
Testifiers	60	26	11	4
Control	61	24	13	1

	LAST ASSAULT TO DISCLOSURE (%)					
	≤ 48 Hours	> 48 Hours– 2 Weeks	> 2 Weeks– 1 Month	> 1 Month– 6 Months	> 6 Months	Unknown
Total	42	17	5	14	15	8
Testifiers	53	16	6	13	9	4
Control	37	21	5	13	15	8

	DISCLOSURE TO REPORT (%)					
	≤ 48 Hours	> 48 Hours– 2 Weeks	> 2 Weeks– 1 Month	> 1 Month– 6 Months	> 6 Months	Unknown
Total	35	23	7	16	16	3
Testifiers	49	20	7	13	9	2
Control	35	25	5	15	16	4

cases were continued by the courts an average of 1.85 times. There were no continuances in some cases, but in others there were as many as 10. The children received an average of 2 subpoenas (range, 0–9).

Case outcomes.—These were of considerable interest, not only for their implications for the children's adjustment, but also because they bear on defendants' fates. In only one case did the defendant plead guilty as charged. It was much more common for a plea bargain to be arranged; this occurred in 126 of the 169 closed cases. Perhaps reflecting DAs' typical stance of prosecuting only strong cases, the courts dismissed only four cases on the basis that no probable cause was found. In two instances, the cases were dismissed on a technicality (i.e., pleading errors). Charges were dismissed by the DA in ten cases; in three of these, it was felt that the allegations against the defendant were false (e.g., the complaining child had several venereal diseases, but the defendant was uninfected, and it was feared that the mother, who was considered an unreliable source, had coached the children). In several of the other cases dismissed by the DA, charges were dropped, but the defendant was prosecuted for similar crimes in stronger cases. We knew of four cases in which the child witness refused to testify and of one in which the child was "unavailable" (e.g., considered too traumatized or mentally unstable to endure testifying).

In 21 cases that went to trial, the defendant was found guilty in 11 instances and acquitted in eight; there were one mistrial and one hung jury.

We were able to obtain data on the defendant's sentence in 133 (out of 138) cases in which a conviction or plea bargain was the final disposition. The defendant received a deferred judgment and deferred sentence in 18 cases and probation without incarceration in 37. The defendant was sentenced to county jail in 24 cases and to prison in 54 cases—in 16 of these instances for more than 8 years.

The harshest judgment was against a defendant who had a long history of sexual and other offenses starting when he was 8 years old. In prison as an adult, he was befriended by a woman who had two daughters. Once out of prison, he started dating the woman and, while dating her, allegedly assaulted the daughters. He was convicted of the child sexual assault charges but, while in jail awaiting sentencing, shot and killed a guard in a foiled escape attempt. By the end of the study, this defendant was sentenced in the child sexual assault case combined with habitual criminal charges to life imprisonment, which in Colorado mandates at least a 40-year term. In the murder case, he was facing the death penalty.

Representativeness of the Sample

The generalizability of our findings rests in part on the representativeness of the subject sample. In total, 61% of the 359 possible families (i.e., who had been referred to the DAs' offices over the 2-year period) participated; given the sensitive nature of child sexual assault cases, we were pleased with this rate of agreement. Nevertheless, the question of whether these cases are representative of the population of child sexual abuse cases referred for prosecution in Denver, Arapahoe, and Adams counties remains. In an attempt to answer it, we collected some data on the families who refused to participate as well as on those we were unable to contact. (The latter occurred mainly when the family's whereabouts were unknown even to the DA's office; thus, prosecution was stymied because the victim could not be found. In three cases, the DAs' offices asked us not to contact the family for fear that this might jeopardize their already tenuous cooperation with the prosecutors.)

Information about the nonincluded cases came from the prosecutors' files and consisted of brief descriptions of the victim, the defendant, the assault, and the charges.

Characteristics of the cases that were and were not included were compared by chi square statistics (see Table 3). Overall, the two groups were comparable in terms of (a) age and race of the victim; (b) age, race, and sex of the defendant; (c) whether the child was injured and, if so, the severity of the injury; (d) the frequency of the abuse; (e) whether the official charge was incest (parental plus other forms); (f) whether a second type of offense was committed against the child (e.g., kidnapping, child physical abuse); and (g) the type of sexual act (e.g., penetration vs. exhibitionism/nongenital fondling).

Nevertheless, the cases included in the study differed from those that were not in several interesting ways. There was a marginal trend for families of older children to decline participation. Surprisingly, proportionally more families of male than female victims agreed to participate; not surprisingly, the relation between the child's relationship to the defendant and the family's participation was inverse: when the defendant was the parent (virtually always the father or stepfather), only 50% of the families agreed to participate, whereas 75% did so when the defendant was a stranger. Differences also occurred as a function of the type of charge filed. If at least one of the formal charges was first-, second-, or third-degree sexual assault, the family was more likely to agree to participate than if that charge was not made. A similar pattern held if one of the charges was sexual assault on a child.[3]

---

[3] In Colorado at the time of this study, *first- and second-degree sexual assault* referred to acts of rape, including penile or digital penetration, fellatio, analingus, etc. These charges could be made with regard to offenses against adult or child victims. First-degree sexual assault typically included more physical force, violence, or threat than did second-degree sexual assault. *Third-degree sexual assault,* which could also be charged for offenses against adults or children, concerned sexual contact other than rape (e.g., fondling). Second- and third-degree sexual assault could include subjecting a child under 18 years of age to sexual

We can only speculate as to the reasons for these differences. Given the sensitivity of cases in which a parent is charged, it is not surprising that proportionally more families declined participation in such instances. Because charges of sexual assault are more likely to be made against non-family members, the same effect may operate here. The child's relation to the defendant may also account for the greater participation of boys' families. In our sample, girls were more likely than boys to be victims of parental incest; given that families were less likely to participate if the father was the defendant, this trend would have excluded more girls than boys. It is also possible that families are more protective of girl than boy victims. Alternatively, if families of boy victims are less likely to report abuse to authorities (Finkelhor, 1984), perhaps those who did so were particularly resilient or unintimidated. In any case, the findings of our study should be considered in light of these differences.

Testifiers and Control Samples

The testifiers and their matched controls represented subsets of the total sample. (Note that the sum of testifiers and control children does not equal 218 because some of the children in the total sample neither testified nor served in the control group.) We describe first how these two groups were established.

Matching.—By the end of the study, we obtained follow-up measures on 55 of 60 children who had testified (the five lost from the study either moved without leaving a forwarding address or did not have a suitable parent or parent substitute to complete the CBCL). Because some designated control children were also lost from the study or became testifiers themselves—and were replaced in either case—75 children served as matched controls. As a result, the composition of the testifier and control group varied as a function of when the follow-up tests were administered. For example, if a child who served in the control group for the first phase of testing was lost from the study before the second phase of testing, the original control child was replaced by another child who had not testified. Thus, the 75 control children and 55 testifiers were never directly compared as groups in our analyses of the matched groups. Rather, at each of the

---

activity when the perpetrator was the victim's guardian or was otherwise in a position of responsibility for the general supervision of the child. *Sexual assault on a child* included subjecting a child to any form of sexual contact when the victim was younger than 15 years of age and the perpetrator was at least four years older than the victim. *Incest,* including aggravated incest, included sexual contact between relatives, such as a parent and a natural child, a child by adoption, or a stepchild, or between a brother and sister, uncle and nephew, etc.

TABLE 3

FREQUENCIES AND CHI SQUARE STATISTICS ON SELECTED VARIABLES FOR PARTICIPATING ($N = 218$) AND NONPARTICIPATING ($N = 140$) FAMILIES

	AGE IN YEARS									
	3–5		6–8		9–11		12–14		15–17	
	N	(%)	N	(%)	N	(%)	N	(%)	N	(%)
Victims:										
Participating....	39	(74)	61	(62)	48	(64)	52	(52)	18	(58)
Nonparticipating....	14	(26)	37	(37)	27	(36)	49	(49)	13	(42)

$\chi^2 = 7.82, df = 4, p < .10$

	SEX			
	Female		Male	
	N	(%)	N	(%)
Participating........	167	(58)	51	(72)
Nonparticipating....	121	(42)	20	(28)

$\chi^2 = 4.01, df = 1, p < .05$

	RACE/ETHNICITY			
	White		Minority	
	N	(%)	N	(%)
Participating........	152	(64)	64	(56)
Nonparticipating....	88	(37)	50	(44)

$\chi^2 = 1.39, df = 1,$ N.S.

TABLE 3 (Continued)

AGE IN YEARS

	18–29		30–39		40–49		50–78	
	N	(%)	N	(%)	N	(%)	N	(%)
Defendants:								
Participating........	74	(69)	76	(68)	39	(72)	24	(67)
Nonparticipating.....	33	(31)	36	(31)	15	(28)	12	(33)

$\chi^2 = 0.42$, $df = 3$, N.S.

SEX[a]

	Female		Male	
	N	(%)	N	(%)
Participating........	6	(67)	214	(60)
Nonparticipating.....	3	(33)	138	(40)

RACE/ETHNICITY

	White		Minority	
	N	(%)	N	(%)
Participating........	134	(64)	82	(57)
Nonparticipating.....	77	(36)	62	(43)

$\chi^2 = 1.28$, $df = 1$, N.S.

RELATIONSHIP TO VICTIM

	Stranger		Acquaintance/ No Position of Trust		Caretaker/ Position of Trust		Parent/ Stepparent	
	N	(%)	N	(%)	N	(%)	N	(%)
Participating..........	14	(74)	59	(62)	94	(67)	51	(50)
Nonparticipating.....	5	(26)	36	(38)	46	(33)	51	(50)

$\chi^2 = 8.75$, $df = 3$, $p < .05$

INJURY

	Yes		No	
	N	(%)	N	(%)
Participating..........	34	(64)	184	(61)
Nonparticipating.....	19	(36)	117	(39)

$\chi^2 = 0.07$, $df = 1$, N.S.

SEVERITY OF INJURY[b]

	Mild		Moderate	
	N	(%)	N	(%)
Participating..........	28	(65)	6	(67)
Nonparticipating.....	15	(35)	3	(33)

$\chi^2 = 0.00$, $df = 1$, N.S.

TABLE 3 (*Continued*)

	FREQUENCY					
	1 Time		Limited		Extended	
	N	(%)	N	(%)	N	(%)
Defendants:						
Participating....	90	(64)	46	(67)	72	(55)
Nonparticipating....	50	(36)	23	(33)	58	(45)

$\chi^2 = 3.28, df = 2$, N.S.

	Yes		No	
CHARGE OF 1ST-, 2D-, OR 3D-DEGREE SEXUAL ASSAULT[c]				
	N	(%)	N	(%)
Participating....	16	(84)	101	(42)
Nonparticipating....	3	(16)	138	(58)

$\chi^2 = 10.86, df = 1, p < .001$

	Yes		No	
CHARGE OF CHILD SEXUAL ASSAULT				
	N	(%)	N	(%)
Participating....	203	(62)	7	(33)
Nonparticipating....	127	(38)	14	(67)

$\chi^2 = 5.45, df = 1, p < .02$

28

	INCEST			
	Yes		No	
	N	(%)	N	(%)
Participating..........	42	(54)	97	(48)
Nonparticipating.....	36	(46)	105	(52)

$\chi^2 = 0.46$, $df = 1$, N.S.

	OTHER OFFENSES			
	Yes		No	
	N	(%)	N	(%)
Participating..........	10	(71)	112	(45)
Nonparticipating.....	4	(29)	137	(55)

$\chi^2 = 2.74$, $df = 1$, $p < .10$

	SEXUAL ACT[d]					
	Nongenital Fondling		Genital Fondling or Oral Sex		Vaginal or Anal Penetration	
	N	(%)	N	(%)	N	(%)
Participating..........	22	(63)	105	(57)	91	(65)
Nonparticipating.....	13	(37)	78	(42)	50	(36)

$\chi^2 = 1.79$, $df = 2$, N.S.

[a] Two cases involved a male and female couple as defendants. Even with these cases added in, expected values were too small to conduct a valid chi square test.

[b] None of the cases were judged to involve severe injury.

[c] For the variables concerning formal charges (e.g., incest). Multiple charges were not uncommon. There were too few cases of attempted sexual assault on a child ($N = 4$) to perform a valid statistical analysis. In one of the nonincluded cases, the charge was unknown.

[d] Nongenital sexual abuse included two cases of exhibitionism as well as cases of nongenital fondling.

29

three follow-ups, different subgroups of these children were compared. Thirteen testifier-control pairs remained the same across all three follow-up assessments.

Each testifier was matched as well as possible with a control child on the following variables: age, gender, initial CBCL total score, relation to the defendant, severity of the abuse, and SES. When possible, the children in each pair were also matched on ethnicity. Given the need to match simultaneously on seven variables, matching criteria could not always be fully met. These criteria and number of exceptions were as follows. (*a*) The children's *ages* had to fall within 2 years, 6 months, of one another (there were three exceptions, with all matches falling within a 3-year, 2-month, range). (*b*) The testifiers' and controls' *initial CBCL total raw score* had to fall within 25 points of each other.[4] Although the majority of matches actually fell within 15 points, there were seven exceptions to the 25-point criterion (the range for the exceptions was 26–45 points). (*c*) The matched pair's *SES* rankings were to fall within 3 points of each other (there were four exceptions, with a range for the exceptions of 4–5 points). (*d*) The child's relationship to the defendant, as assessed on the *SAP relationship-to-defendant scale*, was to fall within two categories of her match (there was only one exception, which differed by 3 points). (*e*) The matched children's scores on the *severity* scale were to be within 4 points (there were seven exceptions, with the exceptions ranging from 5 to 6 points). All pairs were of the same gender; the same *ethnicity* prevailed in 50 cases. We conducted analyses to ensure that the two groups did not differ statistically on the matching variables; their outcome is reported later in this chapter.

It is important to consider why the 75 control children did not take the stand because the reasons might have affected their adjustment and resultant scores on measures that are of central interest in this study. The defendant pled guilty outright in only one of these cases. A plea bargain was arranged in 46 cases; even in these instances, a preliminary hearing had typically been scheduled and then waived or continued one or more times. In many of these cases there appeared to be sufficient evidence (e.g., an admission by the defendant, medical evidence, or a corroborating eyewitness) that the child's testimony was not needed at a preliminary hearing, and the case was then resolved before trial; most of these pleas occurred

---

[4] Raw scores rather than *T* scores were used at the time of matching for the sake of expediency. Matching was not officially conducted on internalizing and externalizing *T* scores; however, because these scores are known to correlate highly with total *T* scores, they are also referred to as matching variables in the present study. How a 25-point difference in raw score corresponds to a difference in total *T* score depends on the child's total number of behavior problems and age/gender group; for the majority (84%) of the children in our study, the difference in total *T* score did not exceed 15 points.

before our follow-up measures were administered. In three cases the defendant was still at large. The charges were dismissed in six cases, one of these after our first follow-up measures were taken. In 15 cases a preliminary hearing and/or trial had been held, waived, or continued without the child having to testify, but the case still remained open, and it was unclear whether the child's testimony would be needed in the future. An additional three children originally used as controls later testified and were reclassified as testifiers. Finally, we were unable to determine why one child failed to testify, but the defendant had already been sentenced before our follow-up measures were administered.

Thus, over half the children in the control sample knew by the time of our follow-up assessments that they would not testify, whereas there was still uncertainty for about one-third of them. To the extent that lack of resolution about testifying might have influenced the latter third's adjustment and thus decreased the likelihood of a control-testifier difference in CBCL scores, our main follow-up analyses are conservative.

Intake assessments were completed for all children as soon as possible after the case was referred for prosecution and once the VAs were able to contact the family; because we did not know who would testify and who would not at the time, it was impossible to match dates for the matched testifiers and controls. Also, the follow-up measures had to be administered on the basis of the point at which testifiers took the stand. A clear event did not mark the start of a comparable period for the control children; however, at the time of the follow-up assessments, testifier and control children were involved in the legal system for an equivalent amount of time (see below). Fortunately, it was also possible to conduct all follow-up assessments of the matched pairs within a circumscribed time period. The 3-month measures were administered within an average of 4.0 days of each other (range, 0–19), the 7-month measures within an average of 4.8 days (range, 0–17), and the final measures within an average of 4.1 days (range, 0–13). At each follow-up, 78% or more of the pairs were assessed within 1 week; across all the follow-ups, the matched-tests assessments were conducted within 2 weeks for all but two pairs (98%).

Testifiers.—Summary information concerning the characteristics of the 55 children is presented in Table 2 above. The demographic characteristics of the victims and defendants are very similar to those of the total sample. The biggest difference lies in the defendant's initial stance: whereas about 40% of the defendants in the entire sample denied the charges, 60% did so in the cases in which the children testified. This difference is predictable given that cases that go to trial are likely to be the most contested. There was also a difference in delays. In the main sample, the proportion of cases in which the child took over 6 months to disclose the abuse and in which it took over 6 months for the disclosure to be reported to authorities was higher in the total sample than in the testifier group. Finally, the main sample contained a somewhat higher percentage of parents and stepparents as defendants than did the testifier group.

The 75 chosen for the control group were also very similar to the total sample (see Table 2). The few differences were that (a) there were more Anglo and fewer Hispanic children and defendants in this group; (b) the total sample contained more cases in which the abuse lasted only 1 day and fewer in which it occurred over a 6-month to 5-year period; and (c) children in the control group were more likely to have suffered no injury and less likely to have suffered a mild one than those in the total sample. Comparisons of the testifier and control groups' characteristics (see Table 2) reveal many of the same differences as those that prevail between the latter group and the total sample.

Comparability of Testifier and Control Groups on Intake Matching Variables

The logic of our study required that the testifier and control children be successfully matched at intake on CBCL scores, age, severity of the abuse, relationship to the defendant, and SES. If, for example, the children's CBCL scores were equivalent at intake but not after the testifiers took the stand, inferences regarding the effects of testifying could reasonably be made. Because the composition of the testifier-control pairs differed at each follow-up, it was necessary to determine whether the testifier-control pairs included in each follow-up were successfully matched.

Three-month follow-up.—The first follow-up was scheduled to occur about 3 months after the child's initial testimony (M = 3 months, 9 days; range = 1 month, 28 days, to 5 months, 10 days) and was obtained on 46 pairs. In this subgroup of testifiers, first testimony was given by 76% at a preliminary hearing, by 2% at a competency hearing, by 4% at a motions hearing, by 15% in trials, and by 2% in sentencing hearings. If a child first testified in a preliminary hearing, it was rare for the case to be closed 3 months later, and often the case was still pending even when the child's first testimony had been at trial. In this subgroup, only seven cases of testifiers and 15 cases of controls had closed (i.e., reached final disposition) by the first follow-up.

First follow-up measures were not obtained for 14 children who had testified, owing to their unavailability or to difficulties in our communications with the DAs' offices; assessments of 13 of these children were obtained at later follow-ups.

To determine if the 46 pairs of testifier and control children differed

TABLE 4

MEAN SCORES OBTAINED BY TESTIFIER AND CONTROL GROUPS AT EACH FOLLOW-UP AND FOR THE LONGITUDINAL
SAMPLE ON INTAKE MATCHING VARIABLES

	FOLLOW-UP							
	3 Months (N = 46)		7 Months (N = 37)		Final (N = 28)		Longitudinal (N = 13)	
MATCHING VARIABLE	Testifier	Control	Testifier	Control	Testifier	Control	Testifier	Control
CBCL T score:								
Total	69.15	68.74	66.97	67.54	67.71	66.25	67.92	68.77
	(10.18)	(10.63)	(11.95)	(10.49)	(11.95)	(9.73)	(8.05)	(8.65)
Internalizing[a]	67.63	66.39	65.05	65.87	65.75	65.32	66.00	66.38
	(8.93)	(9.79)	(9.97)	(9.59)	(9.92)	(8.92)	(6.31)	(7.98)
Externalizing[a]	64.67	66.85	63.30	64.43	63.57	63.57	63.69	65.38
	(9.54)	(9.46)	(10.96)	(9.71)	(11.33)	(9.71)	(8.64)	(7.19)
Age in months	129.35	127.33	125.46	123.16	124.46	126.11	120.00	122.46
	(42.90)	(43.16)	(44.83)	(44.17)	(46.73)	(44.80)	(51.80)	(53.16)
Abuse severity	8.02	7.67	7.97	7.97	8.07	8.04	7.85	8.23
	(2.04)	(1.71)	(1.80)	(1.77)	(1.86)	(1.81)	(2.11)	(1.74)
Relationship to defendant[b]	2.74	2.85	2.84	3.05	2.82	2.93	2.92	3.00
	(.88)	(.87)	(.80)	(.81)	(.90)	(.86)	(.86)	(.91)
SES	4.78	4.83	5.00	4.81	4.89	4.71	4.46	3.92
	(1.85)	(1.65)	(1.63)	(1.73)	(1.59)	(1.49)	(1.76)	(1.44)
Months since disclosure[c]	4.21	4.04	4.58	4.49	4.17	3.96	2.88	4.35

NOTE.—Between-group differences at each follow-up analyzed by F test (see the text); value of F given only when alpha level approached significance. For the matching variables at 3 months, $df = 1.45$; at 7 months, $df = 1.36$; and at the final follow-up, $df = 1.27$. Standard deviations are given in parentheses.

[a] For the 3-month follow-up comparisons: internalizing T scores for testifiers and controls, $F(1.45) = 2.87$, $p < .10$; externalizing T scores, $F(1.45) = 3.68$, $p = .06$.

[b] Relationship to defendant was coded as 1 (stranger), 2 (known to the child but not a caretaker or someone in a position of trust), 3 (known to the child and a caretaker or holding a position of trust but not a parent), or 4 (parent or stepparent).

[c] This variable was analyzed additionally as a between-subjects factor (see the text): $df = 1.90$, at 3 months; $df = 1.72$, at 7 months; and $df = 1.54$, at final follow-up.

at intake on the matching variables, scores from each of the seven matching variables were entered into separate one-way analyses of variance with condition (testifier vs. control) as a blocked variable. As can be seen in Table 4, there were no significant differences between the groups on these measures. The externalizing T score approached significance, with the control children having a higher mean score than the children who testified. Also shown in Table 4 are the findings for a variable called "months since disclosure," by which we mean the number of months elapsed between disclosure of the abuse to authorities and the administration of the first CBCL. Months since disclosure was not used as a matching variable but is important in considering whether children in the two groups had been involved in child abuse investigations for relatively comparable periods of time.

Seven-month follow-up.—We obtained 7-month (M = 7 months, 17 days; range = 6 months, 1 day, to 14 months, 16 days) follow-up measures on 37 matched pairs of children. Considering the children's most recent testimony, 76% testified at preliminary hearings, 8% at competence hearings, 14% in trials, and 2% at sentencing hearings. By the 7-month test, final disposition had been reached for 20 children in the testifier group and 15 children in the control group. The rest of the cases were still in various stages of prosecution.

At the point of the 7-month follow-up, four of the children who had been controls at the first follow-up had testified. A number of other control children were lost from the study and therefore replaced. Because the sample thus differed from that at the first follow-up, one-way analyses of variance on the intake matching variables for this set of children were conducted. These analyses failed to produce reliable effects (see Table 4). In addition, the children did not significantly differ on the number of months since disclosure variable. Thus, the 37 testifier and control pairs included at the 7-month follow-up were successfully matched.

Final follow-up.—By the end of the study, final disposition had been reached for 28 matched pairs of children. By that time, the most recent testimony for the testifiers had taken place for 39% in preliminary hearings, for 7% in competence hearings, for 43% at trial, and for 4% at a sentencing hearing. The final follow-up measures were administered an average of 11 months, 1 day (range = 4 months, 17 days, to 20 months, 11 days), after the child first testified. One-way analyses of variance on the intake matching variables and the month since disclosure variable for the 28 pairs failed to uncover any significant differences (see Table 4).

Longitudinal sample.—Although as a whole the composition of the matched pairs varied across the three follow-up assessments, a subgroup of 13 testifier-control pairs remained constant across all three testings. One-way analyses of variance on the intake matching variables and the month since disclosure variable for these children also failed to uncover any significant differences (see Table 4).

In summary, subsamples of testifier-control pairs were compared on the intake matching variables, and statistically significant differences between the groups failed to emerge. In addition, the matched pairs did not significantly differ in the amount of time that they had been involved in the legal system since they disclosed the abuse. If significant differences in behavioral adjustment were to appear after the testifiers appeared in court, inferences regarding the effect of criminal court testimony could be drawn.

III. THE SEQUENCE OF ASSESSMENTS AND MEASURES

A number of assessments were made, most of them involving parental responses, brief interviews with the children, or courtroom observations. Some were standardized measures frequently used in psychological research, whereas others were developed specifically for the present investigation. Several considerations constrained their selection. None involved asking the victim about the abuse itself. Our agreement with the prosecutors and the families was that we would not pose such questions to the child; this made families more receptive to the study and defense attorneys less likely to subpoena our data. We also selected measures that did not involve extensive interviewing of children (such as psychiatric interviews) since families were typically concerned that the children were already being interviewed too frequently. The measures completed at the courthouse (see Table 1 above) had to be ones that could be administered quickly because the children could have been called to the stand at any moment. The measures are described in the order outlined in Table 1; variables mentioned in this *Monograph* that were derived from the measures are listed in the Appendix.

INTAKE

Informed consent.—At the time of the initial meeting, we obtained informed consent from the child's primary caretaker and assent from the child.

The Sexual Assault Profile (SAP).—We obtained information about the assault from the prosecutors' files, which contained police records and other materials. Parents were also interviewed briefly about the case, and children at times volunteered relevant statements. Such information was recorded on a modified version of Conte and Berliner's (1984) Sexual Assault Profile. As the case progressed and new information became available, the SAP was updated. The profile was filled out by research assistants trained on sample cases at the start of the study and then again midway through. Reliability, assessed by proportion of agreement scores on sample cases, ranged from .63 to 1.00.

The questions on the profile concern demographic information about the child and the defendant (e.g., age, race), characteristics of the abuse (e.g., age at onset, specific acts performed), the child's relation to the defendant, the child's perception of the abuse, the support given by the child's family, other traumas the child might have experienced, etc.

Our main adaptation of the original SAP involved deriving the following summary scales. *The child's relation to the defendant* was coded as 1 (stranger), 2 (known to the child but not a caretaker or someone in a position of trust; e.g., a neighbor), 3 (known to the child and a caretaker or holding a position of trust but not a parent; e.g., a teacher or an uncle), or 4 (parent or stepparent). *Type of sexual activity* involved in the abuse was coded as 1 (exhibitionism), 2 (nongenital contact; e.g., fondling of the child's breasts), 3 (genital contact including oral sex but no vaginal or anal penetration), or 4 (vaginal or anal penetration/intercourse). *Injury to the child* was scored as 1 (none), 2 (mild), 3 (moderate), or 4 (severe). *Amount of force* used was scored 1 (none), 2 (mild), 3 (moderate), or 4 (severe). Force included verbal threats, such as threats to kill the child or the child's mother, as well as more direct shows of force, such as holding a gun to the child's head. *Duration of the abuse* was scored 1 (1 day), 2 (2 days to 6 months), 3 (over 6 months to 5 years), or 4 (over 5 years).

A scale indicating *severity of abuse* was derived by summing the scores assigned to these last four variables. The concept of severity is complex. In addition to the four dimensions we used, many other factors could legitimately enter into the overall concept, such as the child's age at onset and at cessation of abuse, frequency of abuse, age and sex of the accused, and so forth. However, some of these factors, such as duration and frequency of abuse, are likely to be intercorrelated (Browne & Finkelhor, 1986), and others—sex of the perpetrator, for example—are difficult to substantiate as influencing severity because of low base rates (e.g., the number of reported female perpetrators is quite low). Hence, we decided to restrict the concept to a few of the more obvious and quantifiable variables and to examine the others separately.

Two additional scales were derived from the SAP. The families' *perception of threat*, from either the defendant or the defendant's supporters, ranged from 1 (family reports not feeling threatened) to 3 (family reports feeling extreme threat, such as threat of death). The *sentence received* by the defendant if a plea bargain or guilty verdict was obtained was scaled from 1 (deferred judgment or sentence) to 4 (prison).

The Achenbach Child Behavior Checklist (CBCL).—The CBCL served as our main measure of the children's psychological adjustment. The CBCL has been standardized for use with 4–16-year-old children on a wide range of socioeconomic and racial groups and provides norms that permit comparison with others of the same gender and age.[5] The measure consists of Part I, which contains three social competence scales, and Part II, which is more frequently used in research and contains questions concerning internalizing behavior problems (e.g., depression, somatic complaints) and externalizing behavior problems (e.g., delinquency, aggressiveness). The CBCL also provides information that can be used to determine the child's socioeconomic status, on the basis of Hollingshead's seven-step scale (Hollingshead & Redlich, 1958; Watt, 1976).

The psychometric properties of the CBCL are exemplary for scales of this type. For normal children, median short-term (1-week) test-retest reliabilities are both .89; median interrater (mother and father) agreement has been .66. For a clinic sample, mean short-term (3-month), medium-term (6-month), and long-term (18-month) test-retest reliabilities were .74, .65, and .62, respectively; interrater reliabilities ranged from .54 to .87. The validity of the CBCL has been examined as well, showing that its content, construct, and criterion-related validity are all acceptable. For example, scores on all behavior problems and social competence subscales differentiate between clinic and nonclinic children (Achenbach & Edelbrock, 1983) and between abused and nonabused children (Wolfe & Mosk, 1983).

The CBCL was completed by the child's mother in about 80% of the cases, by the child's father in about 7% of the cases, and by other caretakers (e.g., a foster parent, relative, or guardian with whom the child lived) in the remaining cases. The child's behavior was rated as of the last 2 weeks. The children's total CBCL scores as well as internalizing and externalizing subscale scores were converted to T scores using a computer program (see Achenbach & Edelbrock, 1983, app. B) developed by Achenbach and his associates. High T scores represent greater behavioral disturbance. A T score of 63 is recommended as the cutoff between the normal and the clinical range of disturbance for the total score and the internalizing and externalizing scales.

The Teacher Report Form (TRF).—At intake, we obtained parental permission for the child's teacher to complete the TRF (Achenbach & Edelbrock, 1986). This questionnaire is very similar to the CBCL in content and psychometric properties. In studies by Achenbach and Edelbrock (1986), its test-retest reliability averaged .89, .77, and .64 at 1 week, 2 months, and 4 months, respectively. The median short-term (1-week) test-retest reliability for children in special education classes was .90, and the median interrater (teacher and teacher's aide) agreement was .57. Two- and 4-month test-retest reliabilities are available only for 6- and 11-year-old males; these

---

[5] Achenbach and Edelbrock (1986) state that the CBCL can be used with 17-year-olds when necessary.

were .74 and .68, respectively. Content, construct, and criterion-related validity of the TRF have all been found to be acceptable. For example, behavior problem scores differentiate between boys with emotional disorders and boys with learning disabilities (Harris, King, Reifler, & Rosenberg, 1984) and between children referred for services as a result of behavioral or emotional problems and demographically similar nonreferred children (Achenbach & Edelbrock, 1986; Edelbrock & Achenbach, 1984).

The CBCL and TRF are appropriate for longitudinal research and for research in which the questionnaires are completed before and after an intervention (in this case, appearance in court). Like the parents, the teachers were asked to rate the child's behavior over "the last 2 weeks." They were not informed of the child's involvement in a sexual assault case but were told instead that he or she was participating in a study of child development.

The TRF was originally included in our study to assess possible bias in parental reports. We were particularly concerned about incest and boyfriend cases, in which the nonoffending parent might side with the offender and thus blame—or at least feel ambivalent toward—the child. Since the inception of the present study, Achenbach, McConaughy, and Howell (1987) showed that scores on the CBCL and TRF are not highly correlated and hence not interchangeable. These low correlations are attributed by Achenbach et al. (1987) to the fact that parents' and teachers' observations are only partially overlapping since some behaviors are exhibited primarily at home and others primarily at school. Their finding, in addition to the relatively low response rate from teachers in returning our forms, led us to rely almost exclusively on the CBCL.[6]

The Social Adjustment Scale–Self-Report (SAS).—This questionnaire, based on self-report, was used to assess the social adjustment of the child's primary caretaker over the preceding 2-week period. It was included because a child's level of disturbance may depend on the primary parent's

[6] It was still of interest to us to determine the relation between teachers' ratings and ratings by mothers of children involved in incest vs. nonincest cases: if the former were more biased in their judgments, their ratings should be more discrepant from the teachers' ratings than those of the "nonincest-case" mothers. Contrary to this prediction, the correlation obtained at intake between the CBCL total T scores and the TRF scores was .39 for the incest-case group ($N = 16$) and .25 ($N = 74$) for the nonincest-case group. Thus, the formers' ratings were actually more similar to the teachers' ratings than were those of the latter. Achenbach et al. (1987) reported that the average correlation between parents and teachers/observers across a number of studies was .27; however, there was considerable variability across studies, with some correlations falling in the .30–.40 range. Although both the incest- and the nonincest-case mothers' CBCLs thus appear to be within expected limits and roughly comparable, the overall correlation between the parents' and the teachers' total T scores in our study was .27 ($N = 90$), which corresponds exactly to the mean correlation reported by Achenbach et al.

adjustment. The scale includes assessment of the caretaker's relations with her or his children, spouse or partner, and extended family; work and economic circumstances; and overall adjustment. The reliability of the overall adjustment scale is .72 when assessed by interview instead of self-report. Test-retest reliability is also high, $r = .80$. Concurrent validity has been demonstrated (Weissman & Bothwell, 1976; Weissman, Prusoff, Thompson, Harding, & Myers, 1978). High scores indicate greater maladjustment. Weissman et al. (1978) found the mean overall adjustment score for a community sample to be 1.59.

PRECOURT

After obtaining intake measures, we waited to see which of the children were subpoenaed to appear in court, at either a preliminary hearing, a motions hearing, a competence hearing, a trial, or a sentencing. When a child appeared at the courthouse, we greeted the family there and obtained several more measures: Spielberger's State Anxiety Scale (Spielberger, Gorsuch, & Lushene, 1970), the "Before-Court Questionnaire," and an abbreviated form of the CBCL, the "Day-of-Court Measure."

The Spielberger State Anxiety Scale.—The children's precourt anxiety was assessed with this widely used self-report measure. It has high reliability (test-retest, $r = .68$) and validity (see Spielberger et al., 1970; Spielberger, 1973) and is easy to administer. For young children in our study, age-appropriate definitions for some of the test's terms were constructed and used to aid the children. High scores indicate greater anxiety. Spielberger (1973) reports that, based on a normative sample of fourth through sixth graders, the average score was 31.

Before-Court Questionnaire.—The Before-Court Questionnaire was developed specifically for this study and included questions about the child's feelings about testifying, having a nonoffending parent in the courtroom, and testifying in front of the judge, prosecutor, defense attorney, and defendant. A "faces" scale, adapted from Andrews and Withey's (1976) happiness scale and ranging from 1 (very happy) to 4 (very unhappy), was used in eliciting answers. Practice questions (e.g., "What is your favorite food? Point to the face that shows how you feel when you eat your favorite food") were used to ensure that the children understood the scale. The questions were asked by a research assistant (RA) or a victim advocate (VA) who had received appropriate training.

The precourt measure also included sections for the RA or VA to note who brought the child to court, what the child did while waiting, and whether the child toured the courtroom or talked to the prosecutor before being called to testify.

Day-of-Court Measure.—An abbreviated form of the CBCL was used to assess the child's level of disturbance within 48 hours prior to testifying. The form consisted of three categories: questions to assess physical problems such as vomiting, headaches, and dizziness; questions to assess internalizing problems such as nervousness, crying, and clinging behavior; and questions to assess externalizing problems such as fighting, stealing, and temper tantrums. The questionnaire was completed by a nonoffending parent or caretaker at the courthouse while waiting to see if the child's testimony would be required. Responses were provided on a three-point scale ranging from 1 (less than usual) to 3 (more than usual).

COURT

Often, children who were subpoenaed waited around the courthouse for hours, seeming bored and nervous, and then went home without testifying. This occurred when hearings and trials were delayed or "continued" (i.e., set for a later time), defendants waived the hearing or accepted a plea bargain at the last minute, or prosecutors found that the child's testimony was not needed that day. Some of the children did testify, however. We observed each child in the courtroom as she or he underwent direct and cross-examination.

Courtroom Observation Measures.—The Courtroom Observation Measures were also specifically developed for this study. For this measure, ratings were made on 26 scales for the judge's behavior throughout the court session and the child's responses, the prosecutor's behavior and the child's responses during direct and redirect examination, and the defense attorney's behavior and the child's responses during cross- and re-cross-examination. Five overall ratings were made concerning the child's affect generally and toward the defendant specifically as well as the prosecutor's, defense attorney's, and judge's supportiveness of the child. More specifically, the Courtroom Observation Measures focused on the child's responses (e.g., signs of discomfort such as crying, whether the child recanted); the attorneys' questions (e.g., whether the attorney asked mainly about peripheral vs. central events) and demeanor toward the child (e.g., degree of supportiveness); the time course for direct, cross-, redirect, and re-cross-examination (e.g., length of time of cross-examination); the judge's behavior (e.g., whether the judge was supportive); techniques used to aid the child (e.g., use of anatomically detailed dolls); and the presence of others in the courtroom (e.g., whether the courtroom was closed, whether a jury was present). Ratings were typically made on five-point scales; for example, the child's mood while testifying was rated on a scale from 1 (very happy) to 5 (very unhappy). At times, three- or four-point scales were used; for example, the question concerning the child's ability to answer questions was rated on a four-point scale ranging from 1 (answered all questions) to 4 (silent or said only "I don't know"), and the question concerning whether the child cried was rated on a three-point scale ranging from 1 (no) to 3 (a lot). A few of the judgments required dichotomous yes-no responses, such as whether the child recanted the assault.

The observations and ratings were made by one of nine RAs, who were graduate students in psychology, law, social work, or education or nonstudents who held B.A. degrees in psychology. Training was accomplished by having them first make ratings while watching videotapes of children testifying in actual hearings. Interrater reliability was then assessed; once it was .75 or above, pairs of RAs observed children testifying in court. As determined by proportion of agreement scores, this second "training" reliability index was always above .75.

POSTCOURT

After-Court Questionnaire.—The After-Court Questionnaire was administered immediately after children who testified emerged from the courtroom. It was identical to the Before-Court Questionnaire except that the after-court questions were asked in the past tense (e.g., "Now that it's over, how did it feel to testify today?").

THREE-MONTH FOLLOW-UP

Comparison of CBCL scores for testifier and control children 3 and 7 months after the testifiers took the stand and again after the case closed permits inferences about the emotional effects of criminal court testimony on child sexual assault victims. Thus, whenever possible, we obtained a second CBCL from the primary caretaker and TRF from the teacher 3 months after the child testified. By that time we had matched the child who testified with another child whose case had been filed at the prosecutor's office but who had not testified. The CBCL and TRF were also completed for this control child.

SEVEN-MONTH FOLLOW-UP

The seven-month follow-up procedure was identical to that at three months.

FINAL FOLLOW-UP

The CBCL and TRF were again administered after the case officially closed. If a case closed within 7 months of the child testifying, the 7-month and final follow-ups were combined so that only one set of measures was given. (This occurred for 10 pairs of children.) As part of the final follow-up, parents and children were asked to complete a Legal Involvement Questionnaire concerning their impressions of the legal process.

Legal Involvement Questionnaire.—Two questionnaires were developed, one for the child victim and another for the nonoffending caretaker, to assess reactions to the legal system once final disposition of the case (e.g., sentencing, dismissal) was reached. A set of questions was included to verify that the child had or had not testified, how many times she had been interviewed, and whether she had received psychological counseling. Using a total of 19 four-point rating scales (ranging from 1 [very positive] to 4 [very negative] on the caretaker's form and from 1 [very good] to 4 [very bad] on the child's form), the respondent rated her or his feelings about the effects of testifying, the quality of interaction with various legal personnel (e.g., the prosecutor), and the overall effect of legal involvement on her or his life. In addition, respondents rated how satisfied they were with the outcome of the case, how fair and efficient the justice system was, and how informed they had been kept about the course of events (all rated with 1 indicating a positive evaluation and 4 a negative evaluation). A checklist was included on which caretakers indicated whether involvement in the prosecution affected their marital, work, or family relations or their children's behavior. Finally, at the end of the questionnaire, respondents were asked to describe what changes in the legal process they would like to see made. The child's form was a simplified version of the caretaker's form. To make the questionnaire more appropriate for children and less emotionally taxing, the child's version omitted questions about effects on the parents (e.g., on their marital relationship), sentencing, outcome of case, psychological counseling, and how informed the child had been kept about the case.

Case Progress Sheet.—We also recorded a variety of facts concerning the progress of the case through the legal system. These included the total number of continuances; the number of continuances involving court dates for which the child appeared at the courthouse; the number of times the child was subpoenaed, appeared at the courthouse, and testified; the outcome of the preliminary hearing; the length of the legal process, whether the case reached disposition by the end of the study, and, if not, why (e.g., the defendant was still at large, the trial had not yet occurred). In addition, the duration of various time periods was recorded (e.g., time from child's disclosure to the preliminary hearing, time from the preliminary hearing to trial or plea bargain).

IV. THE EMOTIONAL
EFFECTS OF COURTROOM TESTIMONY

The main goal of the study was to determine whether and under what conditions courtroom testimony is associated with child witnesses' emotional distress. After determining that the testifier-control pairs did not reliably differ on the matching variables (see Chap. II), our strategy was to compare caretakers' reports of the testifier and control children's CBCL scores at the three posttestimony follow-up intervals as a function of age, time of test (intake vs. follow-up assessment), and group (testifier vs. control). Because different subgroups of children were included at each follow-up, separate analyses are reported for each assessment. In addition, separate longitudinal analyses are presented for the 13 testifier-control pairs that remained constant across the three follow-up periods. For each of these except the longitudinal analyses, gender was entered into separate analyses that, for lack of sufficient numbers of subjects, excluded age as a factor. These analyses are reported only when significant gender effects emerged, which occurred infrequently.

The CBCL provides a measure of the children's behavioral adjustment but does not explicitly ask caretakers to rate the children's well-being as a result of the prosecution. However, a question concerning the latter was included on the Legal Involvement Questionnaire, on which we obtained caretakers' ratings of whether the child's behavior improved or worsened as a result of participation in the legal process. Analyses of the caretakers' responses to this question after the case closed are also presented in this chapter.

Adverse or positive effects of testifying might appear at some points but not at others. For example, if a child first testified in a preliminary hearing, the case might still be in progress 3 months later, with a trial upcoming and the child in a continued state of anticipation. However, some cases would be resolved (e.g., a plea bargain arranged) after a preliminary hearing, freeing children from further legal involvement. Alternatively, by 7 months some children would have testified more than once, for example, in a preliminary hearing and a trial or in a preliminary and a competence hearing. If testifying repeatedly adds to a child's distress, then one might expect adverse effects to emerge at 7 months rather than at 3 months. Or perhaps children's well-being is affected only while the case is ongoing. If so, one might expect to find adverse effects of testifying at 3 and 7 months but not after the case closed, at which point a subset of children might show positive effects of the experience (e.g., if the defendant was found guilty). However, if testifying has long-term adverse effects on children as a group, negative effects might be evident even after the final disposition of the case. These various possibilities were explored in the sections that follow.

ADJUSTMENT AFTER THREE MONTHS

It will be recalled that we obtained 3-month follow-up data on 46 pairs of children. Each child's total CBCL T scores on the intake and first follow-up were entered into a 3 (age: 4–5, 6–11, and 12–16 years) × 2 (testifier or control group) × 2 (time of test) analysis of variance, with age as the only factor to vary between subjects (see Table 5).[7] The group × time of test interaction was not significant, $F(1,43) = 0.72$; however, all children's scores were higher at intake than at the first follow-up, producing a significant main effect of time of test, $F(1,44) = 7.89$, $p < .01$. Thus, the children's behavioral adjustment improved rather than deteriorated over 3 months regardless of whether they had testified. (The lack of a significant difference between the testifiers' and the control children's scores at the first follow-up was confirmed by a nonsignificant planned comparison and a nonsignificant analysis of covariance with the children's intake total T score used as the covariate.)

However, a significant age × time of test interaction, $F(2,45) = 3.79$, $p < .05$, indicated that significant improvement occurred only for one age group. Post hoc mean comparisons, as calculated by Tukey's HSD test, revealed that the 6–11-year-olds showed significant improvement over time, $p < .01$, whereas the older and younger children did not.

When the age factor was replaced with a gender-of-child factor in a new analysis of variance, the only additional finding was a main effect of gender, $F(1,44) = 5.14$, $p < .05$. Females, $M = 68.74$, SD = 8.64, had higher total T scores than males, $M = 62.02$, SD = 8.34.

A similar pattern of results was obtained when each child's internalizing and externalizing T scores were entered into separate 3 (age) × 2 (group)

---

[7] Age groups were based on Achenbach's scoring system. When the ages of a testifier and control child fell into different groups, classification was determined by the testifier's age; this happened in 11 instances across all three follow-up periods.

TABLE 5

MEAN CBCL SCORES AT INTAKE AND 3-MONTH FOLLOW-UP

	GROUPS			AGE[a]		
	Testifiers (N = 46)	Control (N = 46)	Both (N = 92)	Younger (N = 14)	Middle (N = 38)	Older (N = 40)
Total T score:						
Intake..........	69.15 (10.18)	68.74 (10.63)	68.94 (10.07)	70.64 (12.93)	70.74 (7.64)	66.65 (11.0)
3 months	66.22 (11.64)	64.41 (11.08)	65.32 (8.98)	67.57 (10.17)	64.21 (6.41)	65.58 (10.7)
Internalizing T score:						
Intake..........	67.63 (8.93)	66.39 (9.79)	67.01 (9.04)	68.72 (11.16)	69.40 (7.95)	64.15 (8.88)
3 months	64.67 (9.10)	62.71 (10.20)	63.69 (9.41)	66.07 (9.00)	63.69 (6.09)	62.88 (8.15)
Externalizing T score:						
Intake..........	64.67 (9.54)	66.85 (9.46)	65.76 (8.69)	65.79 (8.68)	68.71 (6.97)	62.95 (9.58)
3 months	63.57 (11.56)	63.04 (9.30)	63.30 (8.20)	67.07 (8.12)	63.00 (7.14)	62.28 (9.15)

NOTE.—Arrows linking italicized scores indicate significant effects ($p < .01$) (see the text). Standard deviations are given in parentheses.

[a] Younger = 4–5 years; middle = 6–11 years; older = 12–16 years.

[b] The indicated effect only approaches significance ($p = .06$).

× 2 (time of test) analyses of variance (see Table 5). A main effect of time of test indicated that the children's internalizing problems decreased from intake to the first follow-up, $F(1,43) = 9.84$, $p < .01$. There were no significant main effects or interactions involving the group factor. In addition, the age × time of test interaction was not significant, $F(2,43) = 2.55$, $p < .10$.

The children's externalizing problems also decreased from intake to the first follow-up, $F(1,45) = 3.26$, $p = .07$, although the effect only approached significance. In addition, a significant group × time interaction emerged, $F(1,43) = 5.36$, $p = .025$ (see Table 5). Simple effects analyses revealed that the control group significantly improved over time, $F(1,45) = 10.63$, $p < .01$, whereas the testifiers did not, $F(1,45) = 0.77$. Nevertheless, the control children's improvement did not result in a significant difference between the groups at the first follow-up, $F(1,45) = 0.07$. Because the control group's initial scores were higher than those of the testifiers, $F(1,45) = 3.68$, $p = .06$, the control group's improvement might simply indicate regression to the mean as opposed to differential improvement across the two groups.

A significant age × time of test interaction, $F(2,45) = 5.57$, $p < .01$, indicated that the improvement was primarily for the middle age group. Post hoc Tukey's HSD mean comparisons revealed that the middle age group's scores were the only ones to show a statistically significant decrease over time, $p < .01$. This group's initial scores were the highest, however. At intake and also at the 3-month follow-up, the scores of the three age groups did not differ reliably: intake, $F(2,43) = 2.26$; 3 months, $F(2,43) = 0.91$. It is interesting to note, however, that, in contrast to the other age groups, the younger children actually evinced a (nonsignificant) increase in their externalizing T scores.

When the age factor was replaced with a gender factor in new analyses of variance, a main effect of gender, $F(1,44) = 5.29$, $p < .05$, indicated that females ($N = 35$), $M = 66.68$, SD = 7.18, had higher internalizing T scores than males ($N = 11$), $M = 61.14$, SD = 7.73. The females' and males' externalizing scores did not differ reliably.

Whether a difference between the testifiers' and the control children's internalizing or externalizing T scores existed at the first follow-up was also explored through planned comparisons and analyses of covariance. These analyses also failed to reveal reliable differences between the groups.

It is also of interest to note that the children's mean intake and 3-month follow-up T scores mostly fell within the clinical range. Thus, the caretakers' reports indicated that, at the time of entry into the criminal justice system, the children were quite distressed and that, although the children's well-being improved, the children at the 3-month assessment were still showing signs of disturbance.

In summary, the general trend was for caretaker report of children's behavioral adjustment to indicate substantial levels of disturbance at time of entry into the criminal justice system but improvement from intake to the 3-month follow-up, regardless of whether the children testified or not. Improvement was most likely to be reflected in 6–11-year-olds' total T and externalizing T scores and least likely to be reflected in the younger children's externalizing T scores. The children's emotional well-being was still precarious at the time of the first follow-up; however, there was little evidence of adverse effects on children of testifying in criminal court.

ADJUSTMENT AFTER SEVEN MONTHS

We obtained 7-month follow-up measures on 37 matched pairs of children. Each pair's total T scores were entered into a 3 (age) × 2 (group) × 2 (time of test) analysis of variance with age as the only between-subjects factor (see Table 6). There were 15, 14, and 8 pairs of children in the older, middle, and younger age groups, respectively. A main effect of time of test, $F(1,34) = 9.08, p < .01$, was subsumed under a significant time of test × group interaction, $F(1,34) = 4.93, p < .05$. The interaction was further analyzed into simple effects. Children in the control group evinced a significant decrease in total behavioral problems from intake to the 7-month follow-up, $F(1,36) = 27.99, p < .001$, whereas children who testified showed less improvement, $F(1,36) = 0.66$. At the time of the 7-month follow-up, the difference in behavioral problems between the control group and the testifiers closely approached significance, $F(1,36) = 3.67, p = .06$. A planned comparison, however, using the mean square error term from the overall analysis revealed a significant effect, $F(1,34) = 8.51, p < .01$. Moreover, analysis of covariance, with the children's intake total T score serving as the covariate, revealed a significant difference between the testifiers' and the control children's 7-month follow-up scores, $F(1,35) = 5.45, p < .05$: testifiers' adjusted $M = 65.46$ and control children's adjusted $M = 60.65$. Thus, control children improved relative to their level of disturbance at intake, whereas testifiers did not.

When the children's internalizing problems T scores were compared, a main effect of time of test, $F(1,34) = 11.64, p < .01$, was again subsumed under a time of test × group interaction, $F(1,34) = 3.82, p = .059$. The children in the control group showed improvement over time, $F(1,36) = 27.12, p < .001$, whereas the children who testified did not, $F(1,36) = 1.36$. Despite these trends, the mean internalizing scores of the two groups did not differ reliably at the time of the 7-month follow-up, $F(1,36) = 2.40$. Again, planned comparisons using the mean square error term from the overall analysis revealed that the latter two means did differ significantly, $F(1,34) = 6.96, p < .05$, as did an analysis of covariance when the children's

TABLE 6

MEAN CBCL SCORES AT INTAKE AND 7-MONTH FOLLOW-UP

| | GROUPS | | | AGE[a] | | |
	Testifiers (N = 37)	Control (N = 37)	Both (N = 74)	Younger (N = 16)	Middle (N = 28)	Older (N = 30)
Total T score:						
Intake...........	66.97 (11.95)	67.54 (10.49)	67.26 (10.82)	66.76 (11.67)	66.50 (11.90)	68.24 (9.99)
7 months.......	65.30 (12.27)	60.81 (10.20)	65.19 (8.75)	61.63 (10.21)	63.43 (9.17)	63.47 (8.09)
Internalizing T score:						
Intake...........	65.05 (9.97)	65.86 (9.59)	65.46 (9.34)	65.26 (10.69)	66.04 (10.96)	65.03 (7.44)
7 months.......	62.97 (11.61)	59.46 (10.02)	61.22 (8.37)	60.07 (9.63)	61.61 (9.29)	61.47 (7.27)
Externalizing T score:						
Intake...........	63.30 (10.96)	64.43 (9.71)	63.87 (9.53)	62.57 (6.61)	65.36 (10.49)	63.17 (10.29)
7 months.......	63.11 (10.46)	60.14 (7.80)	61.63 (7.53)	61.63 (10.03)	63.75 (7.09)	59.64 (6.33)

NOTE.—Arrows linking italicized scores indicate significant effects ($p < .05$ or less) (see the text). Standard deviations are given in parentheses.

[a] Younger = 4–5 years; middle = 6–11 years; older = 12–16 years.

intake internalizing T scores served as the covariate, $F(1,35) = 5.93$, $p < .05$, testifiers' adjusted $M = 63.25$ and control children's adjusted $M = 59.19$.

A very similar pattern emerged when the children's externalizing scores were compared. The time of test × group interaction was significant, $F(1,34) = 4.97$, $p < .05$. The testifiers and control children's scores did not differ reliably at intake. By the second follow-up, the control children's externalizing problems had significantly declined, $F(1,36) = 11.57$, $p < .01$, whereas the children who testified evinced no improvement, $F(1,36) = 0.01$. When the children's scores were directly compared at the second follow-up, the difference was marginally significant, $F(1,36) = 2.87$, $p < .10$. However, planned comparisons using the mean square error term from the overall analysis again indicated significant differences, $F(1,34) = 4.85$, $p < .05$. The analysis of covariance revealed that, when the children's intake externalizing T scores served as the covariate, the difference between the two means was again marginally significant, $F(1,35) = 3.92$, $p < .06$, testifiers' adjusted $M = 63.38$ and control children's adjusted $M = 59.87$.

The analyses of variance described above were also conducted with the age factor replaced by the gender factor. The analyses included 29 pairs of girls and eight pairs of boys. There were no significant main effects or interactions associated with victim gender.

At the 7-month follow-up, the testifiers' average total T score still fell within the clinical range, and their internalizing and externalizing T scores hovered around the clinical cutoff. In contrast, the control children's average T scores all fell within the normal range.

In sum, at the second follow-up, children who did not testify showed improvement in behavioral problems as indexed by all three CBCL scores, whereas children who testified did not.

Possible causes of adverse effects of testifying.—Why did the testifiers exhibit greater disturbance at the second but not the first follow-up? One possible reason is that, by the 7-month test, more of the children had testified at trial. Perhaps trial testimony produces an increase in behavioral disturbance, especially if the case does not close quickly. This possibility was not supported by the data, however; the percentage of children who testified at trial was virtually identical for the first and second follow-ups.

Perhaps the children who testified were more likely than the control children to be involved in open cases by the 7-month follow-up. If prolonged involvement in the legal system leads to greater disturbance (Runyan et al., 1988), the children whose cases were still open should have had higher CBCL scores. To examine this possibility, each child's total T score was entered into a 2 (group) × 2 (time of test) × 2 (case status: open or closed) analysis of variance. A significant three-way interaction would be expected, but none emerged, $F(1,35) = .01$.

Another possibility is that a greater number of the noncontrol children might have testified more than once by the 7-month test. Perhaps multiple court appearances cause an increase in children's emotional disturbance, as do multiple exposures to other stressful events. By the 7-month test, six testifiers had taken the stand twice, whereas the others had testified only once. To examine the effects of testifying more than once, the children's total T, internalizing T, and externalizing T scores were entered into separate 2 (group) $\times$ 2 (time of test) $\times$ 2 (number of times testified: once vs. twice) analyses of variance with number of times testified as the only between-subjects factor. If testifying more than once resulted in greater disturbance, a group $\times$ time of test $\times$ number of times testified interaction should appear.

Mean scores are presented in Table 7. The three-way interaction was not significant in separate analyses of the three CBCL measures. For the total T and the internalizing T scores, the direction of the means is consistent, however, with the prediction that testifying more often results in greater disturbance. Because it was predicted that multiple testimony experiences would lead to greater disturbance, planned comparisons were conducted on the total T scores. Although the intake scores did not reliably differ, children who testified twice had higher total T scores at the 7-month follow-up than their respective controls, $F(1,35) = 6.08$, $p < .025$, and than the children who testified only once, $F(1,35) = 5.38$, $p < .05$. In contrast, the intake and 7-month follow-up scores of the children who testified only once did not differ reliably from those of their controls. Thus, testifying more than once was related to increased disturbance. In fact, children who testified twice showed a slight (nonsignificant) increase in disturbance. Given that none of the children had testified more than once at the 3-month follow-up, the children's increased disturbance at 7 months may have been related at least in part to the fact that several children testified twice by 7 months.

In summary, by the 7-month follow-up, the control children showed significant improvement, whereas the testifiers did not. There was a suggestion in the data that continued behavior problems were associated with repeated courtroom testimony.

ADJUSTMENT AFTER CONCLUSION OF THE CASE

Even though the testifiers showed less improvement than the control children at the 7-month follow-up, it was an open question whether their behavioral adjustment would remain poorer once the children's cases had closed. Perhaps the disturbance shown at 7 months was relatively short lived. By the end of the study, final disposition had been reached for 28 matched

TABLE 7

Mean CBCL Total, Internalizing, and Externalizing Scores for One-Time ($N = 31$) and Two-Time ($N = 6$) Testifiers and Their Controls at the 7-Month Follow-Up

CBCL T Scores

Times Testified/Condition	Total		Internalizing		Externalizing	
	Intake	7 Months	Intake	7 Months	Intake	7 Months
One time:						
Testifiers	66.29	64.00	64.35	61.65	62.74	62.58
	(12.53)	(12.58)	(10.52)	(11.67)	(11.26)	(11.27)
Controls	67.00	60.77	65.58	59.26	64.39	60.39
	(10.63)	(10.00)	(9.71)	(10.27)	(10.13)	(7.54)
Two times:						
Testifiers	70.50	72.00	68.67	69.83	66.17	65.83
	(8.26)	(8.37)	(5.72)	(9.26)	(9.66)	(3.87)
Controls	70.33	61.00	67.33	60.50	64.67	58.83
	(10.19)	(12.25)	(9.63)	(9.42)	(7.92)	(9.77)

Note.—Arrows linking italicized scores indicate significant effects ($p < .05$ or less) (see the text). Standard deviations are given in parentheses.

pairs of children.[8] Each matched pair's total T scores were therefore entered into a 3 (age) $\times$ 2 (group) $\times$ 2 (time of test) analysis of variance with age as the only between-subjects factor (see Table 8). To test the age factor, there were 12, 10, and 6 pairs of children in the older, middle, and younger age groups, respectively. The effect of time of test was significant, $F(1,25)$ = 6.38, $p < .025$. The children's scores dropped between intake and the final follow-up. The group $\times$ time of test interaction was not significant, $F(1,25) = 0.39$. Analysis of covariance using the children's intake total T scores as the covariate also failed to reveal a reliable mean difference between the testifiers' and the control children's final follow-up total T scores, $F(1,26) = 2.28$, testifiers' adjusted $M = 64.27$ and control children's adjusted $M = 61.12$. However, a planned comparison of the testifier and control children's mean scores at the final follow-up indicated a significant difference, $F(1,25) = 4.54$, $p < .05$.

Each pair's internalizing T scores were entered into an analysis of variance as described above. Again, the only significant effect was of time of test, $F(1,25) = 8.99$, $p < .01$. On average, the children's level of behavioral disturbance decreased from intake, $M = 64.16$, to final follow-up, $M = 62.27$, regardless of whether the children testified or not. Because differences were predicted, a planned comparison was performed. By this test, testifiers exhibited a significantly greater number of internalizing problems at the final follow-up than did control children, $F(1,25) = 4.25$, $p = .05$. When the children's externalizing T scores were considered, there were no significant effects. The lack of a reliable effect was confirmed by a nonsignificant planned comparison. Analyses of covariance failed to reveal a significant effect for either the internalizing or the externalizing T scores.

The analyses of variance described above for the final follow-up test were duplicated with the age factor replaced by a gender factor. Twenty-two pairs of girls and six pairs of boys were included in the analyses. There were no significant main effects or interactions associated with gender in any of the analyses.

Possible causes of adverse effects of testifying.—The time between case closing and the final follow-up varied widely (testifiers: 0 months, 15 days, to 16 months, 26 days; controls: 0 months, 8 days, to 18 months, 8 days). This variability permitted us to examine whether case closure or simply time itself influenced the children's well-being. If case closure led to improvement, we reasoned that the children should show improvement relatively quickly after the case closed and that there should be no significant difference between

---

[8] There were two pairs of children for whom the 3-month and final follow-ups or, more likely, the 7-month and final follow-ups were the same; if a pair's case had closed before the 7 months elapsed, the children's scores were entered in both the 7-month and the final follow-up analyses.

TABLE 8

MEAN CBCL SCORES AT INTAKE AND FINAL FOLLOW-UP

	GROUPS			AGE[a]		
	Testifiers (N = 28)	Control (N = 28)	Both (N = 56)	Younger (N = 12)	Middle (N = 20)	Older (N = 24)
Total T score:						
Intake...............	67.71 (11.95)	66.25 (9.74)	66.98 (10.29)	65.67 (8.90)	66.95 (11.91)	67.67 (10.33)
Final follow-up........	64.54 (11.12)	60.86 (7.49)	62.70 (7.51)	59.25 (7.87)	65.40 (7.87)	62.17 (6.81)
Internalizing T score:						
Intake...............	65.75 (9.92)	65.32 (8.92)	65.54 (8.79)	64.83 (8.31)	66.20 (11.00)	65.33 (7.66)
Final follow-up........	62.57 (10.62)	59.21 (7.37)	60.89 (7.30)	58.42 (8.17)	64.05 (8.04)	59.50 (5.78)
Externalizing T score:						
Intake...............	63.57 (11.33)	63.57 (9.12)	63.57 (9.94)	61.67 (6.39)	64.90 (11.22)	63.42 (10.84)
Final follow-up........	62.00 (10.26)	59.64 (7.91)	60.82 (6.96)	59.00 (8.15)	64.50 (6.10)	58.67 (6.25)

NOTE.—Arrows linking italicized scores indicate significant effects ($p < .05$ or less) (see the text). Standard deviations are given in parentheses.

[a] Younger = 4–5 years; middle = 6–11 years; older = 12–16 years.

their scores and those of their matched controls. If instead time is needed, the children should show less improvement relative to their matched controls within a few months after case closure compared to later. To examine these possibilities, the children were divided into two groups: testifiers whose adjustment was measured within 4 months of case closure ($N = 11$) and their matched controls versus testifiers whose adjustment was measured more than 4 months after case closure ($N = 17$) and their matched controls, a division that retained enough children in each group to permit meaningful comparisons. The children's total T, internalizing T, and externalizing T scores were entered into separate 2 (time since case closure) × 2 (group) × 2 (time of test: intake vs. final follow-up) analyses of variance with time since case closure as the only between-subjects factor. The time since case closure × group × time of test interaction was not significant: total T, $F(1,26) = 0.75$; internalizing T, $F(1,26) = 0.13$; and externalizing T, $F(1,26) = 0.01$. The only significant effects were for time of test (i.e., intake vs. final follow-up), with both the testifying and the control children's scores improving over time: total T, $F(1,26) = 6.06$, $p < .025$; internalizing T, $F(1,26) = 8.88$, $p < .01$; externalizing T, $F(1,26) = 2.97$, $p < .10$. Thus, the testifiers whose cases had closed within 4 months showed improvement comparable to those whose cases had been closed for more than four months.

The findings for the 7-month follow-up suggested that a potential stressor for the children was testifying multiple times. By the time their cases closed, 10 children had testified two or more times; 18 children were required to testify only once. Each child's total T score at the final follow-up was entered into a 2 (number of times testified: one vs. two or more) × 2 (group) × 2 (time of test) analysis of variance, with the number of times testified as the only between-subjects factor. The main effect of number of times testified was significant, $F(1,26) = 4.30$, $p < .05$. This finding reflects the fact that total T scores were higher throughout for the children who testified two or more times as well as their matched controls, $M = 68.73$, $SD = 6.46$, compared to children who testified once and their matched controls, $M = 62.68$, $SD = 7.84$. Although the predicted number of times testified × group × time of test interaction was not significant, $F(1,26) = .57$, the pattern of the means at the final follow-up is in accordance with predictions, as can be seen in Table 9. Planned comparisons revealed that, although significant differences did not exist at intake, the children who testified more than once had higher total T scores at the final follow-up than their respective controls, $F(1,26) = 6.65$, $p < .025$, and than the children who testified only once, $F(1,26) = 9.93$, $p < .01$. In contrast, children who testified once did not differ from their controls at intake or final follow-up, $F(1,26) = 2.46$, and $F(1,26) = 3.93$, respectively. The total T

TABLE 9

Mean CBCL Total, Internalizing, and Externalizing Scores for One-Time ($N = 18$) and Two-Time (or More) ($N = 10$) Testifiers and Their Controls at the Final Follow-Up

Times Testified/Condition	Total		Internalizing		Externalizing	
	Intake	Final	Intake	Final	Intake	Final
One time:						
Testifiers	65.00	61.61	63.56	60.39	60.50	60.00
	(13.27)	(11.39)	(10.78)	(10.59)	(11.60)	(10.66)
Controls	64.17	59.94	64.50	58.06	61.50	59.22
	(9.83)	(7.77)	(9.64)	(7.20)	(10.18)	(8.52)
Two or more times:						
Testifiers	72.60	69.80	69.70	66.50	69.10	65.60
	(7.41)	(8.83)	(6.98)	(9.98)	(8.85)	(8.87)
Controls	70.00	62.50	66.80	61.30	67.30	60.40
	(8.81)	(7.04)	(7.73)	(7.57)	(7.97)	(7.03)

Note.—Arrows linking italicized scores indicate significant effects ($p < .05$ or less) (see the text). Standard deviations are given in parentheses.

scores of the children who testified twice remained well within the clinical range, whereas this was not true for the children who testified once.

When the children's internalizing and externalizing scores were analyzed as a function of the number of times the children testified, significant main effects of number of times testified did not emerge: internalizing T scores, $F(1,26) = 2.76$, $p = .10$, and externalizing T scores, $F(1,26) = 3.45$, $p < .10$. In both cases, the nonsignificant trend was for children who testified more than once and their matched controls to evince higher scores throughout ($M = 66.08$, SD $= 6.07$, and $M = 65.60$, SD $= 7.21$, for internalizing and externalizing T scores, respectively) than did the children who testified only once and their matched controls ($M = 61.63$, SD $= 7.15$, and $M = 60.31$, SD $= 7.24$, for internalizing and externalizing T scores, respectively). There were no other significant main effects or interactions. Planned comparisons were consistent with these nonsignificant findings.

Why do children who testify more than once have higher CBCL scores overall? Correlational analyses revealed that two factors were associated with repeated testimony. One was the amount of trauma the child experienced in his or her life after the assault. As traumas, we considered such events as divorce or separation of the child's parents, death of a parent, placement outside the home, or even moving to a new home. Children in the final follow-up group who testified more often had more traumas in their lives than children who testified less frequently, $r = .38$, $N = 26$, $p < .05$. They were also likely to have higher first-time Day-of-Court scores, indicating greater distress 48 hours before having to appear in court, $r = .43$, $N = 22$, $p < .05$. This finding may simply reflect the children's greater overall level of disturbance.

It is unclear why children who are required to testify multiple times have a greater number of traumas in their lives, but correlational analyses indicated several interesting possibilities. During the children's first court appearance, children who experienced more traumas in their lives compared to those who experienced fewer traumas were rated by our court observers as being more credible witnesses during the prosecutor's direct examination, $r = .74$, $N = 18$, $p < .001$, and during the defense attorney's cross-examination, $r = .59$, $N = 17$, $p < .01$. Moreover, cases involving children who had a greater number of traumas in their lives were more likely to be associated with corroborative evidence, $r = .43$, $N = 26$, $p < .025$. For both these reasons, prosecutors might have been more willing to take these cases to trial, requiring more court appearances for the children.

Under the assumption that prolonged legal involvement is likely to be detrimental for children, we predicted that children's behavioral disturbance would be directly related to the number of continuances of the case. Did the children who endured a greater number of continuances show greater disturbance? To answer this question, we first determined whether the children who testified experienced a greater number of continuances than their matched controls. The cases in which the children testified, $M = 2.79$, were continued a greater number of times than the control group's cases, $M = 1.39$, $F(1,27) = 10.00$, $p < .01$. Note that these were continuances of the *case* and may or may not have involved the child's participation. Specifically, we refer here to any type of continuance (i.e., delay) of a court date (e.g., having a preliminary hearing date set for a specific time and then having it delayed to a new date). The greater number of continuances for the children who testified probably reflects the fact that fewer plea bargains were arranged in their cases (eight for testifiers and 23 for controls).

Next, each child's total CBCL T score was entered into a 2 (group) × 2 (time of test) × 2 (number of continuances) analysis of variance. For this analysis, the number of continuances in the testifiers' cases was divided into two groups: cases having zero to two continuances ($N = 12$) and cases having three or more continuances ($N = 16$). This division permitted us to include similar numbers of cases in the two categories. If a greater number of continuances leads to greater disturbance, the testifiers whose cases were continued more often should have exhibited greater disturbance relative to their controls at the final follow-up than the children whose cases were continued fewer times. Mean scores are presented in Table 10. The only significant effect was a main effect of time of test, $F(1,26) = 5.83$, $p < .025$. Analyses identical to the one for the total T scores were conducted on the internalizing and externalizing T scores. The only significant finding was a main effect of time of test for the internalizing T scores, $F(1,26) = 8.38$, $p < .01$. In contrast to prediction, if anything, the children tended to show greater improvement the greater the number of continuances. More continuances of the case may have given children a longer time to improve.

Perhaps it is only continuances that directly involve the child that are retraumatizing. This would seem reasonable given that the child and family might not even know about some of the continuances of the case. The number of continuances that directly involved the child (i.e., in which a subpoena had been sent or the child appeared at the courthouse) did not differ for the testifiers, $M = .11$, and controls, $M = .18$, $F(1,27) = .39$. For children included in the final follow-up group, only three testifiers experienced a continuance that directly involved them, too few to permit us to conduct a valid analysis of variance. It is interesting to note, however, that the testifiers who experienced the continuances actually had lower mean scores than the children who did not (no continuances: intake, $M = 69.16$, SD = 9.49, and final follow-up, $M = 65.72$, SD = 10.38; continuances: intake, $M = 55.67$, SD = 24.58, and final follow-up, $M = 54.67$, SD = 14.57). Perhaps the courts were more likely to agree to a continuance if they felt the child was more stable to start with. It is still possible that children who experience multiple continuances that directly involve them

TABLE 10

MEAN CBCL TOTAL, INTERNALIZING, AND EXTERNALIZING SCORES FOR TESTIFIERS WITH UP TO TWO ($N = 12$) OR THREE OR MORE ($N = 16$) CONTINUANCES (Involving the Child or Not) AND THEIR CONTROLS AT THE FINAL FOLLOW-UP

CONTINUANCES/CONDITION	TOTAL		INTERNALIZING		EXTERNALIZING	
	Intake	Final	Intake	Final	Intake	Final
Zero to two:						
Testifiers..............	65.42	64.25	63.42	63.00	61.67	62.33
	(15.36)	(8.85)	(11.82)	(9.40)	(14.45)	(9.50)
Controls	67.00	61.33	66.25	59.92	63.25	59.17
	(11.08)	(7.58)	(10.23)	(7.25)	(11.35)	(8.18)
Three or more:						
Testifiers..............	69.44	64.75	67.50	62.25	65.00	61.75
	(8.76)	(12.84)	(8.19)	(11.74)	(8.54)	(11.10)
Controls	65.69	60.50	64.63	58.69	63.81	60.00
	(8.93)	(7.65)	(7.64)	(7.64)	(8.68)	(7.95)

NOTE.—Standard deviations are given in parentheses.

will be particularly distressed. We had insufficient data to comment on this possibility.

LONGITUDINAL ANALYSES

The analyses presented above include different subsets of children at the various follow-up tests. This is so for a variety of reasons: some testifiers and control children for whom we obtained first follow-up measures were subsequently lost from the study; some children who were initially used as control children later testified; etc. There was, however, a subset of 13 matched pairs of children whose categories did not change and who were not lost from the study. Because their data were unsullied, it was of interest to conduct analyses that included only these children.

A series of 2 (group: testifier vs. control) × 4 (time of test: intake, 3-month, 7-month, and final follow-ups) analyses of variance was performed, with both factors varying within subjects. For the children's total T scores, a significant main effect of time of test, $F(1,36) = 8.54$, $p < .001$, was subsumed under a significant group × time of test interaction, $F(1,36) = 3.65$, $p < .025$. The interaction was further analyzed into simple effects. The control children evinced significant improvement in their total T scores over time, $F(1,36) = 11.69$, $p < .001$: intake, $M = 68.77$, SD $= 8.65$; 3-month follow-up, $M = 66.54$, SD $= 8.22$; 7-month follow-up, $M = 60.92$, SD $= 8.17$; final follow-up, $M = 61.54$, SD $= 7.76$. In contrast, the testifiers did not show improvement over time, $F(3,36) = 1.40$: intake, $M = 67.92$, SD $= 8.06$; 3-month follow-up, $M = 64.77$, SD $= 9.73$; 7-month follow-up, $M = 67.62$, SD $= 10.55$; and final follow-up, $M = 65.00$, SD $= 11.68$. However, when the two groups were compared at each follow-up point, also through analyses of simple effects, the comparisons were either nonsignificant or only marginally significant: intake, $F(1,12) = 0.38$; 3-month follow-up, $F(1,12) = 3.34$, $p < .10$ (note that the marginally significant difference is for the control children to have higher scores than the testifiers at the first follow-up); 7-month follow-up, $F(1,12) = 4.24$, $p = .06$; final follow-up, $F(1,12) = 0.75$. These trends are consistent with those revealed by the analyses described above, with the largest difference occurring at the 7-month follow-up. Using the mean square error term from the overall analysis of variance, planned comparisons revealed a significant difference at the 7-month follow-up only, $F(1,36) = 10.59$, $p < .01$.

When the children's internalizing and externalizing T scores were similarly analyzed, significant differences emerged for the children's internalizing but not their externalizing scores. Children who testified showed no improvement in their internalizing scores over time, $F(3,36) = 1.51$: intake, $M = 66.00$, SD $= 6.31$; 3-month follow-up, $M = 63.15$, SD $= 8.20$; 7-

month follow-up, $M = 65.31$, SD $= 9.98$; and final follow-up, $M = 62.77$, SD $= 10.34$. In contrast, children who did not testify improved, $F(3,36) = 16.13$, $p < .001$: intake, $M = 66.38$, SD $= 7.98$; 3-month follow-up, $M = 64.62$, SD $= 8.38$; 7-month follow-up, $M = 58.31$, SD $= 8.20$; and final follow-up, $M = 59.00$, SD $= 7.63$. The group $\times$ time of test interaction, $F(3,36) = 4.44$, $p < .01$, from the overall analysis was significant. Simple effects analyses revealed that testifiers had higher scores than control children at the 7-month follow-up, $F(1,12) = 4.98$, $p < .05$, but not at the other three points. The group $\times$ time of test interaction for the children's externalizing scores was only marginally significant, $F(3,36) = 2.33$, $p < .10$. Planned comparisons indicated that, even at the 7-month follow-up, the testifiers' and control children's externalizing scores did not differ significantly.

The longitudinal analyses confirmed that the testifiers did not improve over time whereas the control children did. The lack of improvement for the testifiers is particularly evident at the 7-month follow-up and is reflected in the children's total and internalizing T scores.

CARETAKERS' PERCEPTIONS OF THEIR CHILDREN'S ADJUSTMENTS AS ASSESSED ON THE LEGAL INVOLVEMENT QUESTIONNAIRE

Two items on the Legal Involvement Questionnaire concerned caretakers' perceptions of their children's well-being. These items appeared as part of a checklist in which caretakers were asked to indicate whether involvement in a criminal prosecution affected their lives on a number of dimensions (e.g., work, marital relations, family life). The two items that concerned the child victims' well-being were "child's behavior improved" and "child's behavior worse." The caretakers' responses to these items provided an additional assessment of the children's well-being. Unlike the CBCL, this measure explicitly linked the children's behavior to the criminal prosecution.

There were 24 matched pairs of children from the final follow-up group for whom we obtained completed Legal Involvement Questionnaires. When t tests were performed on the dichotomous yes-no responses for the item concerning children's improvement, the difference between the caretakers' responses for the testifiers and the control children was not significant: caretakers of testifiers, $M = .21$, SD $= .42$, and caretakers of control children, $M = .29$, SD $= .46$. For the item concerning the children's behavior getting worse, the comparison was significant, $t(46) = 2.56$, $p < .025$: caretakers of testifiers, $M = .50$, SD $= .51$, and caretakers of control children, $M = .17$, SD $= .38$. To ensure that the testifiers and control children within this subgroup were comparable, t tests were also conducted to compare the two groups on our matching measures as well as on the measure concerning time since disclosure. None of these comparisons was significant.

In summary, when caretakers were queried as to whether involvement in the criminal prosecution adversely affected their children's behavior, caretakers of testifiers were more likely than caretakers of nontestifiers to answer in the affirmative.

SUMMARY

We compared the testifiers' and the control children's CBCL scores in several ways, and a fairly consistent picture emerged. Three months after the children testified, the behavioral adjustment of the two groups did not differ. In contrast, when tested at 7 months posttestimony, the control group showed improvement, whereas the testifiers did not. By the time of the final follow-up, the testifiers still showed less improvement than the control children, but the effect was considerably weaker than at 7 months. However, after the cases closed, caretaker report of whether the children's behavior improved or worsened as a result of criminal justice involvement, as indicated on the Legal Involvement Questionnaire, also suggested that children who testified were more adversely affected than children who did not. Testifying multiple times appeared to be a stressor and was more likely to be required of children who were already experiencing other forms of trauma in their lives.

V. PREDICTING RECOVERY

One goal of the present study was to identify vulnerability factors associated with adverse effects of legal involvement as well as protective factors associated with beneficial effects. We therefore hoped to discover protective and vulnerability factors that would predict children's improvement or lack of improvement, respectively. For this purpose, improvement was defined in the following way: on the 7-month and then again separately on the final follow-up test, children whose CBCL total T score was equal to or higher than their intake total T score were categorized as children who did not improve. This categorization was based on the following logic: because our previous analyses showed that the general tendency was for children to improve, we included children whose CBCL total T scores remained the same at intake and the 7-month or final follow-up as "nonimprovers," along with children whose scores actually increased. Children whose follow-up total T scores were lower than their initial scores were categorized as "improvers." We did not perform these analyses on the children's 3-month follow-up scores because at that point there was no evidence of negative effects of testifying and because fewer children had completed the entire legal process.

SEVEN-MONTH FOLLOW-UP

At the 7-month follow-up, there were 20 testifiers who improved relative to their intake scores and 17 who did not. Table 11 presents these children's and their matched controls' mean total T scores at intake and at the 7-month follow-up as a function of improvement, group, and time of test. Each child's total T score was entered into a 2 (improvement) $\times$ 2 (group) $\times$ 2 (time of test) analysis of variance, with group and time of test varying within subjects. A significant main effect of time of test, $F(1,35) = 12.28$, $p < .01$, emerged. In addition, a number of two-way interactions were significant: group $\times$ improvement, $F(1,35) = 10.95$, $p < .01$; time of

TABLE 11

Mean CBCL Total T Scores of Testifiers Classified as "Improved" ($N = 20$)
and "Not Improved" ($N = 17$) and Their Controls at Intake and
at the 7-Month Follow-Up

	Time of Test			Time of Test	
Status/Condition	Intake	7 Months	Status/Condition	Intake	7 Months
Improvement:			No improvement:		
Testifiers	70.25	60.05	Testifiers	63.12	71.47
	(10.61)	(10.93)		(12.58)	(11.05)
Controls	70.80	63.45	Controls	63.71	57.71
	(9.29)	(8.92)		(10.79)	(10.99)

Note.—Arrows linking italicized scores indicate significant effects ($p < .01$ or less) (see the text). Standard deviations are given in parentheses.

test $\times$ improvement, $F(1,35) = 21.06$, $p < .001$; and group $\times$ time of test, $F(1,35) = 12.98$, $p < .001$. These main effects and interactions were subsumed, however, within a significant improvement $\times$ group $\times$ time of test interaction, $F(1,35) = 29.03$, $p < .001$.

Analyses of simple effects were employed to investigate the three-way interaction. Testifiers who were defined as having improved and their matched controls had significantly lower total T scores at the 7-month follow-up than at intake: testifiers, $F(1,19) = 23.57$, $p < .001$, and controls, $F(1,19) = 21.24$, $p < .001$. In contrast, testifiers who were defined as not having improved obtained significantly higher total T scores at the 7-month follow-up than at intake, $F(1,16) = 22.38$, $p < .001$, despite the fact that their matched controls showed improvement, $F(1,16) = 8.35$, $p = .01$.

There were initial differences between the groups: the testifiers who showed improvement and their matched controls had higher initial total T scores than did the testifiers who did not show improvement and their matched controls, $F(1,35) = 4.34$, $p < .05$. Nevertheless, by the 7-month follow-up, the behavioral adjustment of all groups but one improved. The testifiers who did not improve had significantly higher total T scores at the 7-month follow-up than did their matched controls, $F(1,16) = 23.96$, $p < .001$. In contrast, the total T scores of the testifiers who improved did not differ from those of their matched controls, $F(1,19) = 1.80$.

Given that a group of testifiers did not improve over the course of their legal involvement, it was of interest to determine whether we could identify child-, family-, or legal-system factors associated with lack of improvement. Correlations were therefore calculated between the many variables in the study and the testifiers' dichotomous improvement scores. The child's age was not significantly related to improvement, $r = -.03$, $N = 32$, but a number of significant correlations emerged, mostly revolving around family and legal factors.

Studies of children's reactions to other stressful events often find that maternal support is an important family-system factor associated with children's resilience. Similarly, children in the present study who had the support of their mothers were more likely to improve, $r = .37$, $N = 29$, $p < .05$. Children who had maternal support were also less likely to have been involved in a concurrent dependency and neglect case, $r = -.44$, $N = 28$, $p < .025$, less likely to be closely related to the defendant, $r = -.37$, $N = 29$, $p < .05$, and more likely to be in families that felt threatened by the defendant or the defendant's family or friends, $r = .46$, $N = 20$, $p < .05$. There was only a marginally significant correlation between the child's relationship to the defendant and the child's likelihood of improving, $r = -.33$, $N = 30$, $p = .07$; the closer the relationship, the less likely the child was to improve.

We predicted that the number of times a child testified would be a legal-system factor associated with distress. Consistent with that prediction, the more often the child testified, the less likely the child was to improve, $r = -.43$, $N = 30$, $p < .025$. This correlation was still significant when the presence or absence of traumas in the children's lives was statistically controlled, $r = -.42$, $N = 28$, $p < .025$. Correspondingly, the more often the child had to appear at the courthouse, the less likely the child was to improve, $r = -.36$, $N = 30$, $p < .05$. (The number of times the child testified and the number of times she or he showed up at the courthouse were highly related, $r = .86$, $N = 30$, $p < .001$.)

Children were more likely to show improvement if they were involved in cases in which there was corroborating evidence to support their claims of sexual assault, $r = .45$, $N = 30$, $p < .025$. (The presence or absence of corroborating evidence was not significantly associated with the outcome of the case or the sentence received, however.)

Finally, caretakers who at the end of the study reported less satisfaction with the legal system, $r = .46$, $N = 19$, $p < .05$, reported feeling that the system was less fair, $r = -.57$, $N = 18$, $p < .01$, and reported that legal involvement had an adverse effect on their child's life, $r = -.48$, $N = 17$, $p < .05$, were more likely to have children who failed to improve.

The correlations given above remained significant when the children's CBCL total T scores at intake were statistically controlled; however, the correlation between improvement and the child's relationship with the defendant, which was only marginally significant to start with, moved even further from significance, $r = -.28$, $N = 29$.

In order to determine the relative weights associated with these predictors, a multiple regression analysis was conducted including the following variables: number of times the child testified, presence or absence of maternal support, presence or absence of corroborative evidence, and relationship to the defendant. (Variables from the Legal Involvement Questionnaire such as satisfaction with the legal system were excluded because the direction of causality was less clear than for the other variables.) The multiple R was high, .73, and significant, $F(4,26) = 7.25, p < .001$. The number of times the child testified was the best predictor of the children's improvement, beta $= -.50, t(26) = 3.61, p < .01$. Maternal support and corroborative evidence contributed about equally to the equation: beta $= .36$ and $.34$, $t(26) = 2.32, p < .05$, and $2.43, p < .025$, respectively. Relationship to the defendant did not enter into the equation. Although the findings are based on a relatively small number of subjects and thus must be interpreted cautiously, the combination of three factors—the number of times the child testified, the presence or absence of maternal support, and the presence or absence of corroborative evidence—accounted for 53% of the variance in the children's improvement.

FINAL FOLLOW-UP

It was also important to determine whether distinct groups of improvers and nonimprovers could be identified at the final follow-up. As noted above, the adverse emotional effects of testifying as indexed by CBCL scores appeared weaker at the final follow-up than at the 7-month follow-up. For the control children and some of the testifiers, improvement occurred by the time the case closed. Nevertheless, a distinct group of testifiers who did not improve could be identified within the group of children who testified, as shown below.

Improvement was again defined solely on the basis of the testifiers' scores. Each child's intake and final total T scores were entered into a 2 (improvement) $\times$ 2 (group) $\times$ 2 (time of test) analysis of variance, with group and time of test varying within subjects. Main effects of group, $F(1,26) = 5.15, p < .05$, and time of test, $F(1,26) = 4.83, p < .05$, were significant, as were the improvement $\times$ time of test, $F(1,26) = 11.16, p < .01$, and group $\times$ time of test, $F(1,26) = 4.93, p < .05$, interactions. A three-way improvement $\times$ group $\times$ time of test interaction was also significant, $F(1,26) = 22.92, p < .001$ (see Table 12).

Simple effects analyses were employed to analyze the three-way interaction. At intake, there were no significant differences as a function of group, $F(1,26) = .33$, improvement, $F(1,26) = 1.02$, or the interaction of these two factors, $F(1,26) = 2.82$. By the time of the final follow-up, control children in both groups showed significant improvement, $F(1,26) = 10.17, p < .01$. As would be expected, the testifiers who were categorized as improvers also evinced significant improvement over time, $F(1,16) = 22.91, p < .001$. In contrast, the testifiers categorized as nonimprovers showed a significant increase in behavioral disturbance over time, $F(1,10) = 7.56, p < .025$. And, of importance, the nonimprovers who testified had significantly higher total

TABLE 12

Mean CBCL Total T Scores of Testifiers Classified as "Improved" ($N = 20$)
and "Not Improved" ($N = 17$) and Their Controls at Intake and
at the Final Follow-Up

STATUS/CONDITION	TIME OF TEST		STATUS/CONDITION	TIME OF TEST	
	Intake	Final		Intake	Final
Improvement:			No improvement:		
Testifiers..........	70.18	56.65	Testifiers	63.91	72.09
	(9.91)	(10.25)		(14.23)	(7.88)
Controls	66.94	61.18	Controls..........	65.18	60.36
	(8.91)	(8.91)		(11.26)	(8.50)

Note.—Arrows linking italicized scores indicate significant effects ($p < .025$ or less) (see the text). Standard deviations are given in parentheses.

T scores at the final follow-up than did their matched controls, $F(1,10) = 12.18$, $p < .01$. Their scores were also significantly higher at final follow-up than the scores of the testifiers who did improve, $F(1,26) = 11.68$, $p < .01$. Thus, we were able to identify a group of 11 children who developed more behavioral problems over the course of their legal involvement. Can we say why?

To explore this question, correlations were calculated between the dichotomous improvement score based on the total T scores at the final follow-up and other variables in the study. In general, child factors (e.g., age, $r = .08$, $N = 26$) and family factors (e.g., maternal support, $r = .29$, $N = 25$) did not predict children's improvement at the time of the final follow-up. The number of times the child testified was also unrelated to improvement, $r = .14$, $N = 28$. One legal factor was significantly associated with improvement: testifiers who improved were *more* likely to have their cases continued than were testifiers who did not improve, $r = .41$, $N = 26$, $p < .05$. This finding was contrary to the prediction that continuances add to the children's distress, but it could be explained in one of two ways. One explanation concerns the possibility that, when a case is continued, the child experiences a sense of relief. Another possibility is that the significant correlation simply reflects the fact that, with time, children generally improved. Thus, the more continuances, the further down the road to recovery the child would be by the time the case closed. Indeed, the correlation between continuances and the length of the legal process was significant, $r = .52$, $N = 25$, $p < .01$, and when the length of the legal process was statistically controlled, the correlation between improvement and continuances was no longer significant. Nevertheless, the correlation between the length of the legal process and improvement was not significant, $r = .31$, $N = 25$, although it might have been given a larger number of testifiers.

There were few other significant predictors of the children's improvement by the time of final follow-up. There was a suggestion in the data that children who feared negative consequences of reporting the abuse were also less likely to improve, $r = -.54$, $N = 13$, $p = .06$, but only two children believed that there would be positive consequences, undermining confidence in the correlation. Caretakers of children who did not improve were more likely to report that the system was unfair, $r = -.42$, $N = 21$, $p < .05$, and that the child's legal involvement had a negative effect on the caretaker's life, $r = -.43$, $N = 22$, $p < .05$. Only two of the significant predictors—the number of continuances and caretakers' perception that legal involvement had a negative effect on their lives—remained significant when the children's intake total T scores were controlled.

It was surprising that several variables discussed in the literature were not significantly related to improvement. For example, 22 of the testifiers for whom we had final follow-up tests received some form of psychological counseling, whereas five did not. (We could not determine whether counseling had taken place for one child.) Psychological counseling was unrelated to improvement, $r = .01$, $N = 25$. Of course, we did not have information on the quality of the counseling received, and the number of children who did not receive counseling was small, so the lack of a significant correlation should be interpreted cautiously.

Tedesco and Schnell (1987) report that repeated questioning of children during the legal investigation is perceived by victims as harmful. We thus expected that the number of times the children were questioned by authorities would be predictive of poorer outcomes. For the testifiers in the final follow-up group, caretakers reported that their children had been questioned from 1 to 10 times ($M = 5$) by authorities, aside from questioning within the courtroom. Caretakers' reports of the number of times their child was questioned by authorities were unrelated to improvement, $r = -.03$, $N = 20$. It should be noted, however, that children in the present study may have been questioned fewer times compared to children whose cases were prosecuted in previous years, given the generally accepted belief that repeated interviewing is stressful for children.

One would think that the disposition of the case would have a substantial effect on children's well-being. For the children in the final follow-up group, five of the defendants were found guilty at trial, eight were acquitted, and eight were involved in plea bargains. In addition, three cases were dismissed by the court, and four were dropped because the child refused to testify, a key witness other than the child was unavailable, or the prosecutor felt that the case could not be proved beyond a reasonable doubt. These various outcomes were combined into a guilty (including plea bargains) versus not guilty (including dismissals and dropped cases) factor, which proved not to be significantly related to children's improvement, $r = .20$, $N = 27$.

If the defendant was found guilty at trial, or if a plea bargain was arranged, the correlation between improvement and the type of sentence received (i.e., deferred judgment, probation, county jail, or prison) approached significance, but in the direction opposite to what might be expected. The more severe the sentence, the less improvement in the child, $r = -.36$, $N = 12$. (As might be suspected, abuse severity and sentencing were reliably related, $r = .58$, $N = 12$, $p < .05$.) When severity of abuse, intake CBCL total T score, or relationship to the defendant was statistically controlled, the correlation between improvement and sentencing was either unchanged or higher (e.g., $r = -.44$, $N = 11$, when severity was controlled), although still nonsignificant. The correlations involving sentencing at trial were based on few children, however.

This finding is worthy of further study as it suggests surprisingly that severe sentencing may not be in the child's best interest. On the one hand, it can be imagined that, if the child was emotionally close to the perpetrator and felt guilty for helping send him or her to jail, a severe sentence might add to the child's distress. On the other hand, it is possible that other variables that correlate with sentencing are responsible for the effect. One likely variable concerns the defendant's history of violence and criminal activity. For example, in one of the cases in which the most severe sentencing occurred, the mother's boyfriend allegedly raped the child, but the mother did not believe the child when she disclosed the assault. The mother continued to see the boyfriend and to have the child interact with him until he was arrested, which occurred after the child disclosed the abuse to another adult. The boyfriend had threatened to kill the child if she told of the rape, and the child feared for her life if he was ever released. The defendant indeed had a past history of violence, including murder. In the middle of the prosecution, the child went to live with her father, and the mother moved out of state. At the time of the final follow-up, the child reported still feeling confused about the legal process and frightened of the defendant. Even though the defendant's sentencing was severe, she stated that, "if he was to get out in the future, I don't know if I could live a normal life without being scared." Thus, it is possible that the positive relation between more severe sentencing and less improvement in the children's adjustment is a by-product of more dangerous offenders being given longer sentences, even if the abuse in the prosecuted case was not as severe as in other cases, at least as indexed by our severity measure.

SUMMARY

We were able to identify subgroups of testifiers who improved and subgroups who did not. When we controlled for initial differences in the groups' behavioral adjustment, a number of factors predicted improvement at 7-month follow-up. These included the number of times the child testified, maternal support, and the presence of corroborating evidence. By the time of the final follow-up, the number of continuances predicted improvement, but the correlation of number of continuances with the length of the legal process suggests that improvement came with time and was actually unrelated to the number of continuances. Caretaker attitudes about the legal system predicted improvement at the 7-month and final follow-ups. Surprisingly, a number of factors that one might expect to be associated with improvement, such as psychological counseling, the outcome of the case, and the number of times the child was interviewed by authorities, were not reliably related to improvement.

VI. AT THE COURTHOUSE

Although our main goal was to examine the emotional effects on children of courtroom testimony, we were also interested in children's attitudes about testifying at the time of the event and the nature of their performance and specific experiences in court. If we are to understand children's reactions to testifying, we need to hear directly from them about their hopes, fears, and anticipations as well as about their suggestions for change. It is also important for us to have a picture of the way they are treated in court and how they react while on the stand. Such observations are relevant to the generalizability of laboratory research on child witnesses. In general, to understand how the child, family, and legal systems interact to influence children's reactions to testifying, we must pinpoint elements of the experience that are particularly frightening for children as well as elements that provide some measure of security or comfort. Innovative techniques to aid children in testifying could then be directed toward reducing children's fears. These issues are addressed in Chapters VI–VIII.

In exploring children's court experiences, we paid particular attention to three child variables (the child's age, gender, and the severity of the abuse) and one family variable (the child's relationship to the defendant). However, we also examined the influence of a number of other family- and legal-system variables, especially those that seemed likely to be associated with the children's attitudes and experiences immediately surrounding and during their court appearances.

WAITING TO TESTIFY

What is it like for children and their families to go to court? Anecdotally, we heard that many families complain about long waits with little diversion for their children. We examined our data on children's activities at the courthouse the first time the children were subpoenaed ($N = 93$) to determine how long they waited and what they did while they waited. On average, the families waited 1 hour, 8 min ($N = 69$), before the child was either called to the stand or sent home. However, the variability was great (range, from 10 min to 6 hours, 15 min); the mode was 3 hours. During the waiting period, the children mainly sat and talked with others (69%) and/or played (40%). Only 15% of the children were shown the courtroom that day. Some of these children had been shown the courtroom on previous days. It was the policy in one of our jurisdictions, however, for children not to receive a courtroom tour. This practice was in response to previous defense arguments that prosecutors had coached children by taking them into court and rehearsing their testimony. (Interestingly, when defense attorneys call child witnesses in support of their clients, a frequent practice is for them also to give the child a courtroom tour; Lipovsky, Tidwell, Kilpatrick, Saunders, & Dawson, 1991.) Recent research suggests that a courtroom tour is generally stress reducing for children (Sas, 1991).

At the courthouse, only 30% of the children sat and talked to the DA about testifying. This is not surprising when one considers that prosecutors had to be in the courtroom arguing their cases at the same time the children were waiting. It was a more common practice for prosecutors to meet with the children before the court date.

The children were typically brought to court by their mothers (65%) or by their mothers and fathers (23%). Fathers alone brought their children to the courthouse in only 5% of the cases. Occasionally, a foster parent (4%), social worker (2%), or female relative (1%) accompanied the child instead of a parent.

BEFORE-COURT MEASURES

Of course, another activity in which the children engaged at the courthouse was completing our measures. Shortly after the children arrived at the courthouse, we interviewed them concerning their feelings about testifying. The interviews were conducted by either the RAs or the VAs. In total, we interviewed 110 children regarding the prospect of their first testimony. This number represents 80% of the children who appeared at the courthouse.

Most of the first precourt interviews (91%) took place on the day of the preliminary hearing, with 5% taking place at competence hearings, 1% taking place at trials, and 3% taking place at other types of hearings (e.g., hearings on motions). The sample consisted of 81 females and 29 males. The children ranged in age from 4 years, 6 months, to 16 years, 9 months ($M = 10$ years, 8 months, SD = 3.38).

The children were asked to provide verbal responses to our questions concerning how they felt about testifying, talking to the judge and the attorneys, having a nonoffending parent present in the courtroom, and seeing the defendant again. Children involved in jury trials were also asked how they felt about testifying before a jury, but so few children whom we could interview testified before a jury that we could not statistically analyze responses to this question. The children's verbal responses to the open-ended questions were coded as positive, ambivalent/neutral, or negative (the "Verbal Scale"). To ensure reliability of this coding, two scorers coded 18% of the interviews. Proportion of agreement scores indicated high reliability, .91. The children also responded to the questions on our "Faces Scale" by pointing to a very happy (1), happy (2), unhappy (3), or very unhappy (4) face as an indication of how they felt. The children's answers to the two response formats were quite similar; verbal responses and responses on the Faces Scale were highly correlated, with r's ranging from .64 to .78, all at $p < .001$.

The children's responses are presented in Table 13, along with chi square values and p levels. For the Verbal Scale, chi squares were calculated by comparing the distributions of the positive and negative responses, ignoring the ambivalent/neutral category. The Faces Scale data were analyzed by combining the "very happy" and "happy" responses and the "unhappy" and "very unhappy" responses.

Note that the number of responses per row does not necessarily add up to 110. This is because children were not necessarily asked and did not

TABLE 13

CHILDREN RESPONDING AT DIFFERENT SCALE LEVELS TO THE PRECOURT QUESTIONS (N = 110)

	SCALE LEVEL					χ^2	p
	+ +	+	0	-	--		
Testifying in court............		18	15	54		18.0	.001
Mother in courtroom		70	7	12		41.0	.001
Father in courtroom		25	1	10		6.42	.025
Talking to judge		32	7	36		.24	. . .
Talking to prosecutor		56	12	10		32.06	.001
Talking to defense attorney....		11	8	45		20.64	.001
Seeing defendant in court		5	8	58		44.58	.001
Testifying in court............	10	20		45	26	16.0	.001
Mother in courtroom	46	29		13	4	36.6	.001
Father in courtroom	20	10		6	3	11.3	.001
Talking to judge	11	39		28	18	.16	. . .
Talking to prosecutor	31	45		17	4	31.2	.001
Talking to defense attorney....	6	15		27	42	25.6	.001
Seeing defendant in court	3	6		28	59	63.4	.001

NOTE.—Items restricted to +, 0, and - were answered verbally and coded as positive, ambivalent/neutral, and negative, respectively (Verbal Scale; see the text); the remainder were answered by pointing to drawings of expressive faces (Faces Scale; see the text) and coded as very happy (+ +), happy (+), unhappy (-), and very unhappy (--).

necessarily answer all the questions. For example, children were generally interviewed only about the nonoffending parent present with them at the courthouse (usually the mother) rather than about both parents. This decision was based on the fact that a substantial number of children were either from single-family homes or involved in an incest case. Another reason for unequal N's is that, at times, children refused to answer certain questions but would answer others. Additionally, we solicited responses only when children evinced an understanding of the question, which was not always the case with younger children. For example, if a child did not know what a defense attorney was and we could not convey the meaning of the term, we skipped this question. Yet another reason was that some children preferred using the Faces Scale and did not want to give a verbal response. Finally, a small proportion of the children's answers were unscorable.

As can be seen, the children generally expressed negative feelings about testifying, about talking to the defense attorney, and especially about having to see the defendant again. The children's attitudes toward the judge were mixed, with some children feeling positively and others negatively. The children expressed generally positive feelings about talking to the prosecutor and about having their (nonoffending) parents, especially their mothers, in the courtroom with them when they testified.

Correlations were calculated between the children's responses to our questions and their age, gender, relationship to the defendant, and the severity of the abuse. Age was significantly related to how the children felt about testifying, with older children expressing more negative feelings than younger children: Verbal Scale, $r = .34$, $N = 83$, $p < .01$; Faces Scale, $r = .35$, $N = 97$, $p < .01$. Using the Faces Scale, older children were also more negative than younger children about the judge and the defense attorney, $r = .27$, $N = 92$, $p < .01$, and $r = .37$, $N = 87$, $p < .001$, respectively. There were no significant correlations associated with the children's responses to the questions on the Before-Court Measure and the children's gender, relationship to the defendant, or severity of the abuse.

It was not unusual for the child to be subpoenaed, appear at the courthouse, and then not testify. But we were particularly interested in examining the data from children who did testify because this enabled us to compare their responses before and after taking the stand. We were able to administer the Before-Court Measure to 39 of the 55 children who testified. Sixteen testifiers were not interviewed for a variety of reasons, including the following. Some children refused to be interviewed. Others, particularly young children in one jurisdiction, were not told why they were at the courthouse. The prosecutors—based again on problems with defense challenges to young children's credibility—encouraged parents not to tell their children why they were there. Since they did not know why they were there, we did not want to be the first to tell them. In a very few cases, we did not know in time that the child had been subpoenaed and either missed the court appearance or arrived too late to administer the various measures.

Thirty-two of the testifiers interviewed were female and seven male. Their age range was identical to that of the larger group of children who were administered the Before-Court Measure, with a mean age of 10 years, 6 months (SD = 3.64). Only 2 of the children testified against a stranger, 14 testified against an acquaintance, 17 against a trusted caregiver, and 6 against a parent. On our severity scale, the children's scores ranged from 5 to 12 (M = 8.03, SD = 1.91).

The testifiers' answers as captured by our Verbal and Faces Scale measures are presented in Table 14. As can be seen, the pattern of responses closely parallels that of the larger group. The children expressed largely negative feelings about testifying in court, about talking to the defense attorney, and about having to face the defendant. The reactions to the judge were again mixed. The children wanted their parents to be in the courtroom and felt positively toward the prosecutor.

Again, the older children were more negative than the younger children about testifying: Verbal Scale, $r = .37$, $N = 30$, $p < .05$, and Faces Scale, $r = .49$, $N = 34$, $p < .01$. They were also more negative about talking to the judge, $r = .42$, $N = 32$, $p < .025$, and to the defense attorney, $r = .60$, $N = 31$, $p < .001$. Again, gender and abuse severity were not significantly related to any of the precourt variables. Since severity of abuse

TABLE 14

FIRST-TIME TESTIFIERS RESPONDING AT DIFFERENT SCALE LEVELS TO THE PRECOURT QUESTIONS ($N = 39$)

	SCALE LEVEL					χ^2	p
	++	+	0	-	--		
Testifying in court............		6	5	21		8.3	.01
Mother in courtroom		30	3	1		27.1	.001
Father in courtroom		6	0	1		...	...
Talking to judge		12	4	9		.4	...
Talking to prosecutor		22	4	1		19.2	.001
Talking to defense attorney....		4	3	18		8.9	.01
Seeing defendant in court		2	2	19		13.8	.001
Testifying in court............	6	4		18	8	7.1	.01
Mother in courtroom	22	9		3	0	23.1	.001
Father in courtroom	4	1		1	1	1.3	...
Talking to judge	6	16		9	3	2.9	...
Talking to prosecutor	10	19		6	1	13.2	.001
Talking to defense attorney....	4	7		9	13	3.7	.10
Seeing defendant in court	1	3		11	19	19.9	.001

NOTE.—Items restricted to +, 0, and - were answered verbally and coded as positive, ambivalent/neutral, and negative, respectively (Verbal Scale; see the text); the remainder were answered by pointing to drawings of expressive faces (Faces Scale; see the text) and coded as very happy (+ +), happy (+), unhappy (-), and very unhappy (--).

showed a marginally significant relation to age, $r = .29$, $N = 37$, $p < .10$, severity of abuse was partialed out of the correlations. The pattern remained the same. Older children were still more negative about testifying: Verbal Scale, $r = .33$, $N = 29$, $p = .07$, and Faces Scale, $r = .45$, $N = 33$, $p < .01$. They remained more negative about talking to the judge, Faces Scale, $r = .39$, $N = 31$, $p < .025$, and to the defense attorney, Verbal Scale, $r = .36$, $N = 22$, $p < .10$, and Faces Scale, $r = .58$, $N = 30$, $p < .001$.

There were no significant correlations between the child's relationship to the defendant and any of the precourt measures. This is surprising because one might expect testifying against one's own parent or stepparent to be more aversive than testifying against a stranger or an acquaintance. The child's relationship to the defendant was associated with the severity of the abuse, however. The more closely related the child was to the defendant, the more severe was the abuse, $r = .33$, $N = 37$, $p < .05$.

SUMMARY

It is clear from these findings that the children initially feared the courtroom and were apprehensive about testifying. Their comments are informative and included statements such as, "I'm scared," "I feel nervous, like everybody is just going to be sitting there staring at me," and "I kinda want to because I want [defendant] to pay for what he did, but I kinda don't want to because I have to say all the stuff he did." The older children were particularly negative about having to go to court, perhaps because they more fully understood the implications of doing so (Melton & Berliner, 1992; Pierre-Puysegur, 1985; Saywitz, 1989; Warren-Leubecker et al., 1989).

What were the children's experiences like once they took the stand? Was it as frightening and aversive as some of them feared? We address these questions next.

When the children were called to the stand, we observed them testify. Our observations offer unique information: as far as we know, there have been no other studies of children's experiences testifying in criminal court. We therefore wanted as complete a description as possible. We were interested in such factors as the child's emotional reaction, the quality of his or her testimony, how the prosecutor, defense attorney, and judge treated the child, how long the child was on the stand, how many people were in the courtroom, and whether any innovative procedures were used to aid the child's testimony. We also wanted to explore whether characteristics of the child, family, and legal systems might be predictive of the child's response.

It should be noted that our observations of the children may not reflect their actual feelings. A child who looks confident might actually feel unnerved; a child who looks relatively relaxed might actually be quite frightened. Our observations of the children are probably best thought of in terms of how the child appeared to the courtroom audience, including the jurors.

Because court procedures differ as a function of the type of court appearance, we conducted separate analyses for preliminary hearings, competence examinations, and trials, the three types of court appearances for which we collected the most data.

PRELIMINARY HEARINGS

Often the child's first and only testimony was at a preliminary hearing. In Colorado, grand juries are not convened in child sexual abuse cases. Instead, a decision about whether the case will be bound over for trial is made by the judge at a preliminary hearing. The preliminary hearing provides both attorneys with their first opportunity to examine the child's in-court credibility. Some professionals fear that defense attorneys will take particular liberty at preliminary hearings to use harsh questioning of child witnesses and thus cause them undue stress and greater apprehension about testifying at trial. This fear is based in part on the assumption that, because a jury is not present, attorneys will take greater liberty in their questioning without fear that jurors will sympathize with the child.

Out of the 218 cases in our study, 128 preliminary hearings were waived, and 89 were held.[9] We could not determine the status of one case. In the preliminary hearings that were held, 46 children testified. We observed 40 of these children (35 girls and 5 boys). It was the first courtroom testimony for all but one of the children. The children ranged in age from 4 to 15 years, with a mean age of 9 years, 9 months (SD = 3 years, 6 months).

Length of testimony and size of audience.—How long were the children on the stand? In the well-known McMartin preschool case, children were questioned at preliminary hearings for weeks at a time, but is this typical? In our study, which did not involve any nationally publicized cases, the children's average time on the stand was 27.5 minutes (SD = 19.13, N = 37), with a range of 4–90 min—considerably less time than might be expected. The prosecutor's direct examination lasted an average of 7.8 min (SD = 4.93, N = 39), whereas the defense attorney's cross-examination lasted an average of 10.3 min (SD = 8.81, N = 38). The judge's questioning of the child lasted on average less than a minute (M = 0.38, SD = 0.92, N = 37), in part because judges, more often than not (i.e., in 30 of 37 cases), did not question the child. Rather, the judge's main interaction with the child was to administer the oath and tell the child to speak up; presumably, the judges were trying to remain as neutral as possible. In 32 of 38 cases, prosecutors did not submit the child to redirect examination; the longest redirect examination we observed lasted only 3 min. Defense re-cross-examination was only observed once in 38 cases and also lasted 3 min. The rest of the time was taken up mostly by interactions between the attorneys and the judge (e.g., discussion of attorneys' objections). Recesses were held for only two of the children, with one of these children being given two recesses.

The number of people present at the preliminary hearing was rated on the following scale: 1 (1–10), 2 (11–20), 3 (21–30), 4 (31–40), or 5 (more than 40). The children generally testified in front of 10–20 people (scale, M = 1.64, SD = 0.38, N = 36), including the judge, attorneys, bailiff, court reporter, and our observer. In three cases, however, there were as many as 30–40 people present.

---

[9] The number of preliminary hearings for which we have data for the Precourt Measures is more than the number for which we have court observations because more children were subpoenaed than testified.

The children's, attorneys', and judges' behavior.—The observers rated the children's overall demeanor as being halfway between "calm" and experiencing "some distress" ($M = 2.51$, SD $= 0.80$, $N = 37$) on a scale ranging from "very calm" (1) to "very distressed" (4). Masked by these overall ratings are 17 children (46%) who showed "some distress" and three (8%) who appeared to be "very distressed." Concerning their apparent reaction to the defendant, the children were rated on average as being halfway between "neutral" and "frightened" of the defendant ($M = 3.35$, SD $= 0.78$, $N = 28$) on a scale that ranged from 1 (very unfrightened of the defendant) to 5 (very frightened of the defendant), with nine (32%) appearing either "very frightened" or "frightened." Of course, these ratings reflect the children's outward appearance and may be more indicative of the impression they made than of their real feelings, a possibility that seems especially likely in light of the children's pre- and postcourt comments about their fears of facing the defendant.

Ratings were also made concerning the prosecutors', defense attorneys', and judges' behavior overall (see Table 15). On average, the prosecutors' demeanor was rated as being "supportive," whereas the defense attorneys' demeanor was rated as being "neutral." Eleven of the defense attorneys were rated as being "unsupportive" or "very unsupportive," however, whereas none of the prosecutors received such ratings. The difference between the supportiveness of the two attorneys was statistically significant.

TABLE 15

CONTRASTS IN MEAN RATINGS OF SUPPORTIVENESS OF PROSECUTOR, DEFENSE ATTORNEY, AND JUDGE

PRELIMINARY HEARING						
Mean		Mean		t	df	p
Prosecutor	1.94 (.77)	Defense	3.06 (1.03)	5.57	34	.001
Prosecutor	1.92 (.76)	Judge	2.63 (.87)	4.40	31	.001
Defense	3.16 (1.00)	Judge	2.61 (.88)	2.65	30	.025
TRIAL						
Prosecutor	1.71 (.85)	Defense	3.12 (.99)	5.80	16	.001
Prosecutor	1.60 (.83)	Judge	2.40 (.63)	3.59	14	.01
Defense	3.12 (1.06)	Judge	2.40 (.63)	2.75	14	.025

NOTE.—Within type of hearing, means for the same legal personnel may differ slightly because of missing data within a comparison. Scale range: 1 = very supportive to 5 = very unsupportive. N for each comparison equals $df + 1$.

The judges received a mean rating that placed them halfway between the prosecutor and the defense attorney. They were viewed as being less supportive than the prosecutors but more supportive than the defense attorneys.

In addition to these overall judgments, separate ratings were made during direct, cross-, redirect, and re-cross-examination. So few children underwent over a minute or two of redirect or re-cross-examination that findings for these parts of the study are not reported. Table 16 presents a variety of comparisons concerning the children's behavior and the attorneys' behavior during direct and cross-examination. As can be seen, several significant differences emerged, but most of them concerned the attorneys' behavior rather than the children's. The children were more likely to answer questions posed by the prosecutor than by the defense attorney but did not appear to be happier, more confident, or more credible under direct than under cross-examination. The defense attorney, however, was judged to focus more on information peripheral or irrelevant to the assault, to use more age-inappropriate wording of questions, and to be less supportive than the prosecutor.

One question that arises in child sexual abuse cases is how often children recant when placed on the stand. During direct examination, one child recanted that the assault occurred, and another recanted the identity of the perpetrator. Three children provided notably inconsistent testimony concerning the actions that took place during the assault, and one of these children and one other child provided inconsistent testimony about peripheral details. During cross-examination, none of the children recanted that the assault occurred or the identity of the perpetrator, although three provided inconsistent testimony about the perpetrator's main actions, and eight of the children provided inconsistent testimony concerning peripheral details. To the extent that jurors focus on inconsistencies in evaluating a witness's testimony, including those concerning peripheral information, some of these inconsistencies could adversely affect a child's credibility (Leippe & Romanczyk, 1987; Wells & Leippe, 1981). In contrast, the general lack of recantation concerning the main assault and the perpetrator's identity would probably be viewed by jurors as a sign of the children's credibility.

Correlations with age, gender, severity of the abuse, and relationship to the defendant.—To examine factors that might be associated with children's courtroom experiences, correlations were calculated between the courtroom observation ratings and the following variables: the children's age, gender, abuse severity, and relationship to the defendant. The intercorrelations of these four variables were all nonsignificant. These variables did, however, significantly relate to the children's experiences on the stand.

We first examined whether any of these factors was associated with the amount of time the children spent testifying. In terms of the total time on

TABLE 16

CONTRASTS IN MEAN RATINGS ON SELECTED COURTROOM OBSERVATION MEASURES OBTAINED DURING PROSECUTION'S DIRECT VERSUS DEFENSE'S CROSS-EXAMINATION AT PRELIMINARY HEARINGS AND TRIALS

	Direct		Cross		t	df	p
	M	(SD)	M	(SD)			
Child's mood (very happy [1]/very sad [5]):							
Preliminary hearing	3.29	(.76)	3.38	(.82)	.90	33	…
Trial	3.41	(1.00)	3.35	(.93)	.27	16	…
Child's confidence (unconfident [1]/confident [5]):							
Preliminary hearing	3.79	(.85)	3.74	(1.02)	.33	33	…
Trial	3.47	(.94)	3.76	(1.09)	1.16	16	…
Child cries (no [1]/a lot [3]):							
Preliminary hearing	1.21	(.55)	1.27	(.57)	.81	32	…
Trial	1.59	(.71)	1.35	(.61)	1.29	16	…
Amount of detail the child provides (none [1]/a lot [4]):							
Preliminary hearing	3.00	(.83)	2.76	(1.03)	1.76	32	…
Trial	3.06	(1.09)	2.47	(1.07)	3.05	16	…
Child answers (silent [1]/all questions [4]):							
Preliminary hearing	1.41	(.56)	1.67	(.54)	2.50	33	.05
Trial	3.65	(.49)	3.24	(.66)	3.35	16	.01
Child recants assault (no [0]/yes [1]):							
Preliminary hearing	.00	(.00)	.00	(.00)	.00	32	…
Trial	.00	(.00)	.00	(.00)	.00	16	…
Child's credibility (low [1]/high [4]):							
Preliminary hearing	3.47	(.62)	3.35	(.69)	1.28	33	…
Trial	3.41	(.51)	3.29	(.59)	1.46	16	…
Attorney's focus (assault [1]/irrelevancies [3]):							
Preliminary hearing	1.00	(.00)	1.61	(.56)	6.27	32	.01
Trial	1.53	(.72)	2.06	(.56)	2.73	16	.05
Attorney's questions (age inappropriate [1]/appropriate [5]):							
Preliminary hearing	4.62	(.78)	4.12	(.91)	4.40	33	.01
Trial	4.88	(.33)	3.71	(1.11)	4.51	16	.01
Attorney's demeanor (supportive [1]/unsupportive [5]):							
Preliminary hearing	1.91	(.75)	3.00	(.95)	5.45	33	.01
Trial	1.71	(.85)	3.12	(.99)	6.20	16	.01

NOTE.—Preliminary hearing, N = 33–34; trial, N = 17.

the stand, only one correlation was significant: boys spent more total time on the stand than girls, $r = .36$, $N = 37$, $p < .025$. None of the four variables was significantly associated with the length of direct examination. During cross-examination, older children underwent longer questioning than younger children, $r = .34$, $N = 38$, $p < .01$, whereas the severity of the case was only marginally related to the amount of time the child was placed under cross-examination, $r = .26$, $N = 38$, $p < .06$. The amount of time the child was questioned during redirect examination was significantly associated with two factors: the child's relationship to the defendant and the child's credibility during cross-examination. The more closely related the child was to the defendant, the longer the child was questioned, $r = .31$, $N = 38$, $p < .05$. When the child appeared to be a less credible witness during cross-examination because, for example, she provided inconsistent testimony concerning the defendant's main actions during the assault or inconsistent testimony concerning information peripheral to the assault, redirect examination was more drawn out, $r = -.41$, $N = 34$, $p < .01$, presumably because the prosecutor attempted to rehabilitate the child's credibility.

In addition to the time measures, we also examined correlations of the children's age, gender, and relationship to defendant, as well as abuse severity, with our measures of the children's courtroom experiences. The children's age played a role in both direct and cross-examination. During direct examination, age was significantly related to the children's demeanor, $r = .43$, $N = 36$, $p < .01$, with the older children appearing to be sadder than the younger children. Perhaps they better appreciated the seriousness of the proceedings. During cross-examination, cognitive and/or intimidation factors associated with age were influential: compared to older children, the younger children's speech was more faltering, $r = .35$, $N = 35$, $p < .05$, they provided less detail, $r = .44$, $N = 34$, $p < .01$, and they appeared to be less credible witnesses, $r = .34$, $N = 35$, $p < .05$. This latter finding is contrary to reports in the experimental literature (Duggan et al., 1989; Goodman et al., 1989).

The child's gender was also related to several of our measures. The prosecutors' questioning was more likely to focus on central information concerning the assault for girls than for boys, $r = .42$, $N = 35$, $p < .025$. Boys were more likely than girls to testify in front of a larger audience, $r = .39$, $N = 36$, $p < .025$.

The child's relationship to the defendant was related to how angry the child appeared to be toward him or her, $r = -.46$, $N = 31$, $p < .01$, with the children showing more sympathy to the defendant the closer the relationship. The child's relationship to the defendant was directly related, however, to how uncooperative the child was with the defense attorney, $r = .39$, $N = 35$, $p < .025$. That is, the closer the child's relationship to the defendant, the less cooperative the child was while being questioned by the defense attorney. The child's behavior might well have been influenced by the defense attorney's posture toward the child, which was judged to be more hostile the closer the child's relationship to the defendant, $r = .29, N = 35, p < .05$. When the relationship was close, the children were less likely to have a nonoffending parent or other loved one in the courtroom, $r = -.33, N = 39, p < .025$, and were less likely to testify with the aid of props, $r = -.28, N = 37, p < .05$.

The severity of the abuse was also significantly related to several variables. The more severe the abuse, the more confident the child, $r = .28, N = 36, p < .05$, the more fluent the child's speech, $r = .30, N = 36, p < .05$, and the less likely the child was to provide inconsistent testimony concerning the perpetrator's main actions during the assault, $r = -.30, N = 36, p < .05$, during direct examination. When the abuse was severe, the defendant was more likely to be seated out of view, $r = .39, N = 37, p < .01$, but the child's nonoffending parent/loved one was less likely to be permitted to remain in the courtroom, $r = -.32, N = 39, p < .025$, as were other people in general, $r = -.29, N = 36, p < .05$. Also when the abuse was severe, other stressors were more likely to occur, $r = .34, N = 33, p < .05$, such as the child being cross-examined by the defendant instead of the defense attorney, vomiting while waiting to testify, or seeing other witnesses emerge from the courtroom crying.

Typically, the judges played a passive role in the preliminary hearings, to an extent that made scoring of their behavior difficult. Therefore, the judge's behavior was coded only if the judge took active steps to talk to the child or intercede, which occurred in only relatively few cases. When it did occur, the judges' behavior was influenced by the severity of the abuse. In the severe cases, the judge was more likely to ask questions that went to the child's competence (e.g., questioning the child about truth and lies), $r = .71, N = 9, p < .025$, less likely to ask the child for clarification of an answer, $r = -.71, N = 9, p < .025$, and more likely to take steps to protect the child, $r = .42, N = 19, p < .05$, such as having the defendant sit out of view. Although the judges' demeanor was generally neutral toward the children, when it was not, the judges were less supportive toward boys than girls, $r = .87, N = 7, p < .01$. Not surprisingly, the judges asked the younger children more questions concerning competence, $r = -.76, N = 9, p < .025$. But, given the relatively few cases that contributed to these correlations, the findings should be considered suggestive rather than definitive.

Innovative practices.—Despite laws in Colorado that permit the use of a variety of innovative techniques designed to decrease courtroom trauma to child victims in sexual assault cases (e.g., videotaped testimony), use of these techniques was infrequent. The three most common methods employed to protect the children at preliminary hearings were having the VA sit in the

TABLE 17

INCIDENCE OF INNOVATIVE TECHNIQUES USED AT PRELIMINARY HEARINGS AND AT TRIALS

	Preliminary Hearing	Trial		Preliminary Hearing	Trial
Sitting on lap of supportive adult....	1 (3)	0 (0)	Testimony over closed-circuit television..........	1 (3)	0 (0)
Parent/loved one in courtroom	18 (46)	5 (29)	Defendant out of view..............	3 (8)	2 (12)
VA in courtroom.....	31 (80)	16 (94)	Courtroom cleared ...	17 (45)	1 (6)
Taking toy to stand ...	4 (11)	5 (30)	Testimony in judge's chambers ...	2 (5)	0 (0)
Testifying with aid of props	4 (11)	9 (53)	Other	3 (8)	2 (12)
Videotaped testimony	0 (0)	0 (0)			

NOTE.—Percentage of preliminary hearings or trials in which the innovative technique was employed is presented in parentheses. The N varies from 37 to 39 for preliminary hearings and from 16 to 17 for trials.

audience, closing the courtroom to spectators, and permitting the child's nonoffending parent/loved one to remain in the courtroom (see Table 17). These techniques all involve attempts to reduce the child's intimidation through the presence of a support person or the absence of onlookers.

Other techniques were used relatively infrequently. Sitting on a supportive other's lap is often objected to by defense attorneys out of fear that the child's testimony could be surreptitiously influenced. Indeed, it was permitted at a preliminary hearing in only one case. A few children, usually the youngest ones, were permitted to take a toy to the stand and to testify with the aid of props (e.g., anatomically detailed dolls). Only one child testified over closed-circuit television, and none of the children testified on videotape. For three of the children, the defendant was out of view, and two of the children testified in judges' chambers. Finally, three children were given the benefit of another type of innovative procedure, such as having the tables in the courtroom rearranged so that the child was seated further from the defendant.

That relatively few innovative procedures were employed can be explained by several facts. Prosecutors have been hesitant to use certain innovative techniques (e.g., videotaped testimony) for fear that such procedures will be ruled unconstitutional. Moreover, some prosecutors expressed concern that the use of techniques such as testimony via videotape or closed-circuit television would reduce the judge's or jury's sympathy for the child. Some techniques can be used only in certain situations (e.g., after a showing that the child would be too traumatized to testify otherwise). Some judges are persuaded by defense objections to the techniques and thus rule against them despite prosecutors' requests.

Use of innovative techniques has been controversial owing to fears that they infringe on defendants' rights. However, child advocates have argued that innovative techniques are necessary to elicit the most complete and accurate testimony from children and to reduce the stressfulness of testifying. We had also predicted that innovative techniques would be associated with more complete testimony and less fearfulness. Although use of innovative techniques was generally infrequent at preliminary hearings, several were used often enough to permit examination of their relation to the children's responses in court; specifically, we could examine having a parent/loved one or a VA in the courtroom and having the courtroom cleared of spectators.

The presence of a nonoffending parent/loved one in the courtroom, which was not significantly related to the children's age, was associated with the children's responses. Children were judged to be less frightened of the defendant throughout their testimony if the parent/loved one remained in the courtroom, $r = -.39, N = 28, p < .025$. Also, during the defense attorney's questioning, children whose parent/loved one remained in court were also less likely to provide inconsistent testimony regarding peripheral details, $r = -.35, N = 34, p < .025$, and more likely to be judged credible witnesses, $r = .34, N = 35, p < .05$. These correlations maintained significance when abuse severity and relationship to defendant (both related to the parent/loved one being permitted to remain in the courtroom) were statistically controlled.

Several significant associations were uncovered between the children's responses and the presence of a VA in the courtroom. Because presence of a VA was associated with the child's age, $r = .24, N = 39, p = .07$, age was partialed from the following correlations. When children appeared to be more fearful, they were more likely to have a VA present in the courtroom, $r = .34, N = 33, p < .05$. The presence of a VA was associated with the child being less likely to recant the identity of the perpetrator, $r = -.38, N = 33, p = .025$, and less likely to recant main actions of the perpetrator during defense questioning, $r = -.37, N = 32, p < .05$.

Clearing the courtroom of spectators was also associated with the children's age; the courtroom was more likely to be cleared if a young child testified, $r = -.29, N = 38, p < .05$. Whether or not age was statistically controlled, clearing the courtroom was associated with the children being less likely to cry during defense questioning, $r = -.33, N = 34, p < .05$.

Neither the presence of a VA nor clearing the courtroom was significantly associated with the child's gender, relationship to defendant, or abuse severity.

In summary, although few innovative practices were used, the few we could evaluate were associated with child witnesses being less likely to recant previous testimony, less likely to be frightened or tearful (with the exception of an association between fright and VA presence), and more likely to be viewed as credible witnesses.

COMPETENCE EXAMINATIONS

In Colorado, children called to testify as victims in sexual abuse cases are presumed to be competent witnesses regardless of age. Nevertheless, in preliminary hearings and trials, the prosecutors' initial questions during direct examination often addressed the children's competence. The children might be asked, for example, if they knew the difference between the truth and a lie and what would happen if they told a lie. These questions were presumably asked to satisfy the judge, defense attorney, and the jury that the children were competent to testify.

Despite the presumption of competence, an attorney can always challenge the competence of a witness. This occurred for eight of the children (seven females and one male), who then testified at hearings specifically held to determine their competence as witnesses. The children ranged in age from 5 to 8 years ($M = 6$). When a competence hearing occurred, it was usually held after the preliminary hearing but before the trial. Therefore, five of the eight children we observed had already testified before the competence examination was held.

The children were questioned from 4 to 21 min ($M = 10.63$, SD $= 5.93$). In contrast to the preliminary hearings, in which the judge played a passive role, the judge was a more active figure in the competence examination. The judge's questioning lasted 5.75 min, on average (SD $= 2.61$). In most of the cases, the attorneys did not do any of the questioning. When they did, their questioning lasted only 3–8 min.

Seven of the eight hearings were held in the judges' chambers. Regardless of where the hearing was held, the defendant was present and in view in all cases. Six of the hearings were closed to the public, but even when hearings were not officially closed, it was "local custom" to limit the number of people permitted to enter the judges' chambers and therefore, in effect, to close the courtroom to spectators. For seven of the eight hearings, no more than 10 people were present when the child testified. In five cases, the child's parent was among those present. Most (six) of the children were also permitted to take a toy with them while they testified. A VA was present for half the children, and this was more likely to occur for younger than for older children.

Overall, the children's demeanor was judged to be midway between "calm" and "very calm" ($M = 1.6$, SD $= 0.52$, $N = 8$) on the continuum "very calm" (1) to "very distressed" (4). None of the children cried, although one child was judged to be "very frightened of the defendant." The judges were rated as "very supportive" (M = 1.13, SD = 0.35, N = 8). Given that most of the attorneys did not ask any questions, data were too sparse for any other meaningful statements about their behavior.

The observers rated the children's performance as either "credible" (3) or "highly credible" (4) on a four-point credibility scale (M = 3.62, SD = 0.52, N = 8), and the judges generally agreed. Seven of the eight children were judged to be competent witnesses.

Given that so few children experienced a competence hearing, we refrained from conducting further analyses of these data.

TRIALS

When most people think about a child testifying in court, they think of testimony at trial rather than at preliminary hearings or competence examinations. In fact, trials are much less frequent than preliminary or grand jury hearings, but when they are held, they are more formal and dramatic, with the rules of evidence strictly dictating the proceedings. A jury is frequently present, and its members—or the judge if the trial is to the court—must be convinced beyond a reasonable doubt of the defendant's guilt. Thus, considerable tension surrounds a trial.

Of course, many cases never reach the trial stage but are instead resolved through plea bargaining. In our study, only 21 cases went to trial. Nineteen children testified in these trials.

There is considerable lore about how attorneys, particularly defense attorneys, question children at trial. On the one hand, especially if a jury is involved, defense attorneys may be hesitant to question a young child harshly, for fear that jury members will sympathize with the victim. On the other hand, it is possible that older children might be treated more like adult rape victims, who often feel that they are put on trial along with the defendant. Children lack their own representation at trial, so they are not guaranteed protection: the prosecutor represents the state, not the victim. Nevertheless, it is generally in the prosecutor's interest to protect the child, if not out of concern for the young witness, then to promote the child's performance on the stand.

We observed 17 of the 19 children (12 girls and 5 boys; M = 11 years, 4 months, SD = 4 years, 4 months, range 5–17 years) testify at trial. The trial date marked the first time two children testified, the second time nine children testified, the third time five children testified, and the fourth time one child testified.

Length of testimony and size of audience.—On average, the children spent

69 min on the stand, but with considerable variability (SD = 56.92). One child spent only 13 min testifying, whereas another spent more than 4½ hours over a 2-day period. On average, direct and cross-examination lasted 30 min (SD = 25.30) and 32 min (SD = 30.43), respectively. Fourteen of the children experienced redirect examination, which lasted 3.29 min on average (SD = 2.55). Only four children experienced re-cross-examination, which lasted 3.5 min on average (SD = 1.54). Thirteen of the children were not questioned by the judge except to be greeted, given the oath, and at times asked if they were comfortable or to speak up. Seven of the children were not given a recess, but all the others experienced at least one, and one child experienced eight.

Fifteen of the children testified in jury trials. Regardless of whether the trial was to a jury or to the court (i.e., the judge), the defendant was always present in the courtroom. On average, the children testified in front of 21–30 people (scale M = 3.00, scale SD = 0.61), although three of the children testified before 31–40 people.

Children's, attorneys', and judges' behavior.—Overall, the children's mood was judged to be midway between "calm" and "some distress," but 11 (65%) of the 17 children were rated as experiencing "some distress" or as being "very distressed." Concerning the children's overall fear of the defendant during the trial, our raters felt that they could make a judgment only for 10 children. On average, these children appeared to be neutral toward the defendant (M = 3.10, SD = 1.29), although 30% of the children were rated as frightened or very frightened.

The mean overall ratings for the supportiveness of the prosecutor, defense attorney, and judge are presented in Table 15 above. As was true at preliminary hearings, the prosecutor was rated as the most supportive and the defense attorney as the least supportive of the three. The judges' level of supportiveness again fell between that of the prosecuting and defense attorneys.

Many of our findings regarding trials are consistent with those regarding preliminary hearings. As before, the children's behavior remained fairly constant throughout the proceedings, with the attorney's behavior differing more consistently (see Table 16 above). The children answered fewer of the defense attorneys' than the prosecutors' questions, and when they did answer, they provided the former less detail. Nevertheless, the children on average appeared to be equally happy or sad, competent, and credible regardless of which attorney questioned them. None of the children recanted the abuse, and they were as likely to cry during direct as during cross-examination. In contrast, the attorneys' behavior differed in a number of ways. As we found at the preliminary hearings, the defense attorneys compared to the prosecutors were judged to focus more on peripheral information than the assault, to ask questions in a less age-appropriate manner, and to be less supportive.

Correlations with age, gender, abuse severity, and relationship to the defendant.—Correlations between the courtroom measures and the child's age, gender, abuse severity, and relationship to the defendant were calculated. The intercorrelations between these latter four variables were nonsignificant except that the more severe cases were more likely to involve a close relationship between the child and the defendant, $r = .52, N = 16, p < .05$. The relation between the child's age and the severity of the abuse was marginally significant, $r = .42, N = 16, p = .10$.

The two main factors related to the children's experiences on the stand were age and severity of the abuse. This can be seen, for example, for the time measures. The length of time the children were on the stand was significantly related to their age, with the older children being questioned for longer total periods of time, $r = .64, p < .01$, and also for longer periods of time during direct examination, $r = .63, p < .01$, and cross-examination, $r = .64, p < .01$, than the younger children ($N = 17$ for all these correlations). These correlations remained significant when abuse severity was statistically controlled.

The time factors were also related to the severity of the assault, with the more severe cases requiring more total time on the stand, $r = .64, p < .05$, and more time for direct examination, $r = .61, p < .05$, cross-examination, $r = .59, p < .05$, and redirect examination, $r = .72, p < .01$ ($N = 16$ for all these correlations). However, the correlations concerning direct and cross-examination were no longer significant when age and relationship to the defendant were statistically controlled. There were no significant correlations between the time measures and the child's relationship to the defendant or the child's gender. Thus, the total amount of time the child was on the stand was related to both the child's age and the severity of the abuse. The length of direct and cross-examination was more strongly related to the child's age than to severity, whereas the length of redirect examination was primarily related to severity, not age.

The child's age was significantly related to a number of other variables as well. Overall, the prosecutors and the defense attorneys were less supportive of the older than the younger children, $r = .66, p < .01$, and $r = .68, p < .01$, respectively ($N = 17$ in both cases), whereas the judges' overall demeanor did not vary reliably with the child's age, $r = .25, N = 15$. During direct examination, the older children appeared to be sadder than the younger children, $r = .50, N = 17, p < .05$, but this relation was due in part to the severity of the abuse; it was no longer significant when severity was controlled, $r = .41, N = 13$. During direct examination, older children could answer a greater number of the prosecutors' questions, $r = .53, p <$

.05, and provide more detail, $r = .69$, $p < .01$, than the younger children ($N = 17$ in both cases). During cross-examination, the older children were again more likely to provide greater detail in response to the questions, $r = .57$, $N = 17$, $p < .05$. These significant relations were maintained when severity was statistically controlled. Contrary to prediction, the correlation between age and the children's perceived credibility was nonsignificant: direct examination, $r = .30$, and cross-examination, $r = .01$ ($N = 17$ in both cases). If anything, during direct examination, older children were seen as more credible witnesses than younger children.

In sum, both types of attorneys were more supportive of the younger children, but, even so, the younger children's cognitive abilities or level of intimidation kept them from testifying in as great detail as the older children.

A similar pattern appeared for redirect examination, experienced by 14 children. In terms of the attorneys' demeanor, the prosecutor was again more supportive of the younger than of the older children, $r = .73$, $N = 14$, $p < .01$. In terms of the extent of the children's testimony, the younger children could answer fewer questions and were thus more likely to remain silent, $r = .78$, $N = 12$, $p < .01$, or to provide less detail when they did answer a question, $r = .73$, $N = 14$, $p < .01$, than the older children. One difference in the pattern at redirect compared to direct examination was that the younger children now appeared to be sadder than the older children, $r = -.68$, $N = 14$, $p < .01$. Perhaps by this point the younger children's energy was beginning to wane, they were feeling more intimidated, or they better understood the implications of the event. Again, these correlations were still significant when severity was controlled. There were too few children who experienced re-cross-examination to calculate valid correlations.

The severity of the assault was also related to the children's experiences. Regardless of age, children involved in more severe cases were more likely to appear sad and cry during cross-examination, $r = .48$, $N = 16$, $p = .05$, and $r = .65$, $N = 16$, $p < .05$, respectively; be asked more questions not focused on the assault by the prosecutor during redirect examination, $r = .61$, $N = 11$, $p < .05$; and provide greater detail during redirect examination, $r = .65$, $N = 11$, $p < .05$. When relationship to the defendant was controlled, these relations remained significant.

The child's relationship to the defendant was significantly related to only one of our courtroom observation measures: regardless of severity, prosecutors focused more on the main assault when the defendant was less related to the child, $r = .55$, $N = 16$, $p < .05$. When the defendant was a stranger or acquaintance and the child's interactions with him or her were presumably of a more limited nature, prosecutors would have had less of a tertiary nature to question the children about; when the defendant is known, additional concerns (e.g., motivation to fabricate) might need to be addressed. Gender was not significantly related to the children's experiences as assessed by any of the courtroom measures.

Innovative techniques.—The use of innovative techniques to help the children testify was relatively rare (see Table 17 above). The most common techniques employed at trial involved allowing a support person (nonoffending parent/loved one or VA) in the courtroom and permitting the child access to props, either toys for comfort or aids to testimony (e.g., a blackboard). Predictably, the younger children were more likely to take a toy to the stand for comfort, $r = -.70, N = 17, p < .01$. In general, the most common innovative techniques used at trial differed from those used at preliminary hearings. Even the most consistently used technique—the presence of a support person—differed somewhat across the two types of proceedings. Whereas the support person was more likely to be a VA than a nonoffending parent/loved one at both types of proceedings, a smaller percentage of nonoffending parents/loved ones were present at trials than at preliminary hearings.

At trial, none of the children sat on the lap of a loved one, and none of them testified via videotape or closed-circuit television. The defendant was seated in the courtroom but out of view in two of the trials, both involving younger children. In contrast to preliminary hearings in which the courtroom was not infrequently closed to spectators, the courtroom was closed in only one trial. A few of the children were given the benefit of other procedures, such as having the defendant seated in view but further away from the child than usual, and this was more likely to occur when the child's relationship to the defendant was close, $r = .60, N = 16, p < .001$, regardless of severity. Given the small number of children who were exposed to other procedures, the replicability of these significant correlations must be questioned.

Again, because most innovative practices were infrequent, we were limited in our ability to explore their effects. And, because the one frequently used innovation—the presence of a VA in the courtroom—occurred for virtually every trial, there was insufficient variability to examine the influence of the VAs' presence. However, we did conduct analyses to explore relations between the children's responses and three innovative practices: a nonoffending parent/loved one remaining in the courtroom, the child taking a toy to the stand, and the child testifying with the aid of props.

If a nonoffending parent/loved one was permitted to remain in the courtroom with the child, the child was able to answer a larger number of the prosecutors' questions, $r = .48, N = 17, p = .05$. Whether the parent/loved one was present was unrelated to the child's age, abuse severity, or relationship to the defendant.

Because age and relationship to the defendant, $r = -.57, N = 13, p$

< .05, were both significantly related to taking a toy to the stand, these variables were statistically controlled in the following analyses. Prosecutors were less likely to use leading questions when children had a toy, $r = -.67$, $N = 12, p < .01$. During cross-examination by the defense attorney, children with a toy were more likely to recant previous testimony concerning peripheral details, $r = .57, N = 11, p < .05$. Taking a toy to the stand was not significantly related to abuse severity or gender.

During direct examination, children were more likely to use props to help them testify if their speech was faltering, $r = -.57, N = 17, p < .05$. During cross-examination by the defense attorney, children who testified with props were more likely to recant previous testimony concerning peripheral details, $r = .63, N = 16, p < .01$, and to be less uncooperative with the defense attorney, $r = -.48, N = 17, p < .05$; also, the defense attorneys' demeanor toward the child was less hostile, $r = -.50, N = 17, p < .05$. Whether the child used props was unrelated to the child's age, abuse severity, or relationship to the defendant.

In summary, aside from the presence of a VA in the courtroom and the use of props to aid the children in testifying, innovative practices were infrequently employed at trial. Presence of a parent/loved one was associated with children answering more questions during direct examination. Taking a toy to the stand and using props were both associated with the child recanting previous testimony about peripheral details; perhaps the toys were somewhat distracting for children. Taking a toy to the stand and using props were associated with changes in attorneys' behavior, but we can only speculate as to why. When a child held a toy, prosecutors avoided leading questions, perhaps fearing that the toy would emphasize the children's youth and potential suggestibility to the factfinder. When children used props, defense attorneys were more supportive of the children, perhaps again because the props emphasized the children's youth; defense attorneys would not want to appear insensitive to young witnesses. However, the small number of children who testified weakened our statistical power to uncover significant effects; thus, the lack of a significant relation should not be interpreted as evidence for or against the use of innovative courtroom practices.

BEFORE-COURT AND SELECTED SAP MEASURES

In the analyses presented above, age, gender, abuse severity, and relation to the defendant were considered, but several other variables were also of interest, such as the child's level of precourt anxiety and fear of the defendant, the amount of maternal support the child received, and the amount of threat the child and family experienced. For these analyses we considered the children during their first court appearance. This choice permitted us to include the largest number of children possible (47) without confounding the analyses with children who testified repeatedly.

One question concerned how the children's responses to our precourt questionnaires—the Spielberger State Anxiety Scale, the Day-of-Court Measure, and the Before-Court Measure—related to children's experiences on the stand. In different ways, each of these measures assessed the children's anxieties about testifying. If such measures could be used to identify children who would have a more difficult or traumatic experience testifying, they might prove useful to the courts.

On the Spielberger State Anxiety Scale the children's mean score was 41.26 points. For sake of comparison with Spielberger's norms, we calculated the 9–11-year-olds' mean score, which was 41.61 (SD = 12.45, N = 38); compared to Spielberger's mean score of 31 for a normative sample of similarly aged children, the children awaiting court were expressing anxiety.

The child's mean score on the Spielberger State Anxiety Scale was not reliably related to the child's age, gender, or relationship to the defendant. It was, however, correlated with the severity of the assault, $r = .31, N = 42, p < .05$. Children who experienced more severe assaults expressed the most anxiety on the day they were to testify.

The children's mean Spielberger score was significantly related to the focus of the prosecutors' questions, $r = -.34, N = 38, p < .05$, with prosecutors focusing less on irrelevancies when the children were very anxious; perhaps prosecutors feared that the more nervous children would not last through longer questioning. The children's credibility during direct but not cross-examination was also related to the mean Spielberger score, $r = .34$, $N = 39, p < .05$, with the more anxious children appearing to be more credible witnesses. Adults, including our raters, may expect child victims to be nervous on the stand and may use the child's nervousness as an index of credibility. Both these correlations were only marginally significant, however, when severity was controlled.

The Day-of-Court Measure, completed by the parent who accompanied the child to court, assessed the child's behavioral disturbance 48 hours before the court date. The Day-of-Court Measure was predictive of the child's ability to answer the prosecutor's questions, $r = -.34, N = 35, p < .05$, with the children who evinced greater disturbance being less able to answer the prosecutors' questions. All the correlations presented above concerning the Spielberger State Anxiety Scale and the Day-of-Court Measure remained significant when age was statistically controlled.

It was also of interest to examine whether the children's responses to our Before-Court Measure were related to their experiences in court. When age was statistically controlled, the children's general precourt attitude about testifying (our first precourt question) was not significantly related to their courtroom experiences. In contrast, the children's attitudes about testifying in front of the defendant were reliably associated with their ability to answer the prosecutors' questions, $r = -.41$, $N = 40$, $p < .025$, and to provide a detailed response when they did answer, $r = -.45$, $N = 40$, $p < .01$. The children who were most upset about testifying in front of the defendant had a more difficult time answering the prosecutors' questions.

In addition to examining how measures of the children's anxieties related to their court experiences, we were also interested in determining whether maternal support, an important family-system factor, would help bolster the children and make the experience of testifying easier for them. Surprisingly, the amount of maternal support the children received at the time of disclosure or during the legal process was unrelated to their courtroom experience.

However, the extent to which the families reported feeling threatened was related to the children's testimony. Children from families experiencing a greater sense of threat either from the defendant or from the defendant's supporters (e.g., defendant's family or fellow church members) were judged to be more credible during direct and cross-examination than children from families reporting less threat, $r = .63$, $N = 25$, $p < .001$, and $r = .55$, $N = 24$, $p < .01$, respectively. When perceptions of threat existed, children had reason to be nervous, and, indeed, they appeared more frightened on the stand, $r = .50$, $N = 21$, $p < .025$. (Interestingly, the children's and families' sense of threat was not reliably related to the severity of the actual assault as we measured it.) These correlations remained significant when age was statistically controlled.

SUMMARY

In summary, the two main determinants of the children's courtroom experiences were age and severity of the assault. Younger children had a more difficult time answering the attorneys' questions. In contrast, children involved in more severe cases were able to recount more about the abuse. A number of factors that one might predict would have a pervasive influence on the children's experiences did not, such as maternal support, relationship to the defendant, and gender. The small number of boy victim/witnesses who testified may have made it difficult to find significant gender differences, however.

In addition to age and severity, intimidation played a role. How the children felt about testifying in front of the defendant was associated with the children's ability to answer the prosecutors' questions. Moreover, when the children and families reported having felt threatened by the defendant and his or her supporters, the children appeared to be more anxious on the stand. This anxiety actually appeared to be beneficial, however, to the children's perceived credibility.

Not surprisingly, the prosecutors were judged to be more supportive of the children than were the defense attorneys. Nevertheless, the younger the child, the more supportive both attorneys became. Compared to defense attorneys, prosecutors asked questions in more age-appropriate language and centered their questions on the main aspects of the assault.

Some notable gender differences in the children's experiences during preliminary hearings were uncovered. At these hearings, judges were less supportive of boy than girl victim/witnesses. The boys testified longer and in front of a larger audience than the girls. Given that only five boys testified, these findings must be interpreted cautiously, however.

Except during competence examinations, judges generally played a passive role. With only a few notable exceptions, they did not take active steps to protect the child. Judges' mandate to appear objective and fair by not favoring one side over the other probably dictated their relative passivity.

Relatively few innovative techniques were used to make the children more comfortable or aid them in testifying. Aside from having the VA (who was at times a near stranger to the child) sit in the courtroom, the majority of the children testified as would adults. At preliminary hearings compared to trials, parents were more likely to remain in the courtroom, and the courtroom was more likely to be cleared. At trials compared to preliminary hearings, a greater percentage of children took a toy to the stand or used props, including anatomically detailed dolls, to help them testify. As we had predicted, presence of a support person was associated with a number of beneficial effects (e.g., children being less fearful, more able to answer questions, and less likely to recant); clearing the courtroom was associated with less crying. Presence of toys or props, however, was associated with recantation of peripheral details during cross-examination.

How did the children feel once they emerged from the courtroom? After the children testified, we interviewed them once again. In all but two cases, the questions were the same as those used on the Before-Court Measure, although they were now asked in the past tense. The two exceptions concerned the children's parents. These questions were changed to reflect the fact that parents were not always permitted to be in the courtroom while the child testified. We thus asked the children how they felt about the parent being or not being in the courtroom, as was appropriate.

We were able to interview 38 of the children ($M = 11.6$ years, range 4.5–16.6 years, SD = 3.69) immediately after they first testified. We were not able to interview 17 children for a variety of reasons. Some children refused to be interviewed. Some had families who, after what was typically an emotionally taxing day, decided to go home as soon as possible. Some children were too distressed (e.g., one child was crying uncontrollably because, after she testified, her parent fainted in the hallway and paramedics arrived by ambulance to take the parent to the hospital). Occasionally, we had not been informed of the child's court appearance, in which case we attempted to obtain answers to the After-Court Measure questions within 48 hours of the court appearance.

Twenty-eight of the children had testified at preliminary hearings, four at competence examinations, four at trial, and two at other types of hearings such as motions hearings. Four of the children had testified against a stranger, 13 against an acquaintance, 13 against a trusted caregiver, and 8 against a parent or stepparent. On our severity of abuse measure, the children's scores ranged from 5 to 14 ($M = 7.97$, SD = 2.10).

Table 18 presents the number of children who responded to each question on the Verbal and Faces Scales of the After-Court Measure. In contrast to the precourt responses, the children as a group no longer felt as negative about testifying. In general, the positive responses resulted from the children finding the event less aversive than they had feared, although some of the positive responses seemed mainly to indicate that they were just

TABLE 18

TESTIFIERS RESPONDING AT DIFFERENT SCALE LEVELS TO THE POSTCOURT
QUESTIONS (N = 38)

	SCALE LEVEL					χ^2	p
	+ +	+	0	-	--		
Testifying in court............		14	10	9		1.1	...
Mother in courtroom:							
Mother present.............		11	2	2		6.24	.05
Mother not present.........		4	0	6		.40	...
Father in courtroom:							
Father present		0	0	0		...	...
Father not present.........		2	1	2		...	...
Talking to judge		23	1	1		20.2	.001
Talking to prosecutor		18	2	3		10.7	.01
Talking to defense attorney....		7	5	13		1.8	...
Seeing defendant in court		3	1	21		13.5	.001
Testifying in court............	11	6		11	6	.0	...
Mother in courtroom:							
Mother present.............	12	4		1	2	8.9	.01
Mother not present.........	2	2		4	4	8.0	.05
Father in courtroom:							
Father present	1	1		0	0	...	...
Father not present.........	1	1		1	3	...	...
Talking to judge	13	20		1	0	30.1	...
Talking to prosecutor	14	15		5	0	16.9	.001
Talking to defense attorney....	6	8		10	6	.1	...
Seeing defendant in court	2	2		14	16	19.9	.001

NOTE.—Items restricted to +, 0, and - were answered verbally and coded as positive, ambivalent/neutral, and
negative, respectively (Verbal Scale; see the text); the remainder were answered by pointing to drawings of expressive
faces (Faces Scale; see the text) and coded as very happy (+ +), happy (+), unhappy (-), and very unhappy (--).

glad it was over. There was still, however, a substantial subgroup who were
unhappy about the experience. When asked about the judge, the over-
whelming majority of children now felt positively, whereas on the Before-
Court Measure there had been a distinct bimodal distribution. Those children whose mothers were permitted to remain in the courtroom still felt
positively about having them present. Those children whose mothers were
excluded from the courtroom were unhappy about it, at least as indicated
on the Faces Scale. The children also remained positive about talking to the
prosecutor. Although the majority of the children still felt negatively about
talking to the defense attorney, a substantial number of them now felt positively about it. Despite the general trend for the children to become more
positive in their responses, there was one question that still elicited largely
negative feelings: even after the fact, children were still quite unhappy
about testifying in front of the defendant.

For the After-Court Measure, correlations of the children's Verbal and
Faces Scale responses with the children's age, gender, and relationship to

the defendant as well as the severity of the abuse were calculated. Consistent with precourt findings, the older children were still more negative about testifying, $r = .46$, $N = 32$, $p < .01$ (Faces Scale), and about the defense attorney, $r = .57$, $N = 23$, $p < .01$ (Verbal and Faces Scale), and $r = .52$, $N = 28$, $p < .01$ (Faces Scale), than were the younger children. In addition, the older children felt worse testifying in front of the defendant, $r = .57$, $N = 23$, $p < .01$. Gender also made a difference, with females expressing more negative feelings than males about having testified in front of the defendant, $r = -.36$, $N = 32$, $p < .05$ (Faces Scale).

Because age and severity of abuse were intercorrelated, $r = .31$, $N = 35$, $p < .06$, second-order correlations were computed, partialing out severity. Still, the older children felt more negatively than the younger children about testifying, $r = .45$, $N = 31$, $p < .01$ (Faces Scale). The older children again expressed more negative feelings about the defense attorney, $r = .54$, $N = 21$, $p < .01$ (Verbal Scale), and $r = .46$, $N = 27$, $p < .025$ (Faces Scale). Finally, the older children still expressed more negative feelings about having to face the defendant, $r = .59$, $N = 22$, $p < .01$ (Verbal Scale).

There were no significant correlations between the children's responses on the After-Court Measure and their relationship to the defendant or the severity of the abuse.

BEFORE- VERSUS AFTER-COURT COMPARISONS

Given that we had both Before- and After-Court Measures on a subset of the same children, we were able to compare their responses on the two interviews. Mean scores for the children on the two measures are presented in Table 19, along with the results of a series of two-tailed t tests for matched samples. By the time the After-Court Measure was administered, the children overall had become more positive about testifying, more positive about the judge, and more positive about the defense attorney. Compared to their desire to have their mothers in court with them, the children whose mothers were excluded from the courtroom were unhappy about it. Their feelings remained largely unchanged about the prosecutor. The negative feelings about testifying in the defendant's presence remained strong even after testifying. In fact, the most negative ratings were elicited by the question about testifying in front of the defendant.

CHILDREN'S SUGGESTIONS FOR CHANGE

The children were also asked, "Was there anything that would have made you feel better about testifying today?" We scored the children's an-

TABLE 19

DIFFERENCES IN MEAN SCORES OF FIRST-TIME TESTIFIERS ON THEIR RESPONSES TO
QUESTIONS ASKED ABOUT PRE- VERSUS POSTCOURT EXPERIENCE ($N = 38$)

	VERBAL SCALES[a]				
	Precourt	Postcourt	df	t	p
Testifying in court............	2.58	1.83	23	3.89	.001
	(.72)	(.82)			
Mother in courtroom:					
Mother present............	1.18	1.45	11	.09	...
	(.41)	(.82)			
Mother not present	1.29	2.43	6	1.92	...
	(.76)	(.98)			
Father in courtroom	...	...	...	...	...
Talking to judge	1.88	1.17	16	2.78	.025
	(.99)	(.53)			
Talking to prosecutor	1.06	1.23	16	1.38	...
	(.24)	(.56)			
Talking to defense attorney....	2.76	2.05	16	3.17	.01
	(.56)	(.90)			
Seeing defendant in court	2.75	2.69	15	.72	...
	(.58)	(.70)			
	FACES SCALES[b]				
Testifying in court............	2.89	2.26	26	2.94	.01
	(.89)	(1.13)			
Mother in courtroom:					
Mother present............	1.33	1.80	14	1.33	...
	(.72)	(1.08)			
Mother not present	1.56	2.78	8	2.63	.05
	(.73)	(1.20)			
Father in courtroom	...	...	...	...	...
Talking to judge	2.24	1.60	24	3.72	.001
	(.83)	(.58)			
Talking to prosecutor	1.89	1.59	26	1.99	.10
	(.64)	(.69)			
Talking to defense attorney....	3.05	2.45	19	2.85	.01
	(.95)	(1.05)			
Seeing defendant in court	3.38	3.23	25	.94	...
	(.70)	(.91)			

NOTE.—N for each comparison equals $df + 1$. Standard deviations are given in parentheses.
[a] 1 = positive; 2 = neutral/ambivalent; 3 = negative.
[b] 1 = very happy; 2 = happy; 3 = unhappy; 4 = very unhappy.

swers according to 10 categories (e.g., close the courtroom to spectators, permit closed-circuit television or videotaped testimony, fewer continuances). These categories were developed on the basis of existing literature and the children's actual responses. If a child's responses fell into more than one category, all appropriate categories were scored. When we again restricted our analysis to children who testified for the first time, 18 of the 38 were unable or unwilling to respond to this question. For those who did respond, the most frequent answer concerned the presence of the defendant in the courtroom. Ten of the 20 children (50%) said they would have preferred the defendant to be absent. The next most frequent response, given by six children (20%), was that, despite a desire for some changes, the experience was acceptable the way it was. The nonoffending parent of 12 of the children was excluded from the courtroom. Three (25%) of these 12 children complained that their parent should have been present in the courtroom. These findings should be considered in light of the fact that children, especially young ones, may have a difficult time verbalizing their feelings and fears and that many of the children just seemed glad that the experience was over.

SUMMARY

In contrast to the children's precourt attitudes, once the children testified, they generally found the ordeal to be less aversive than they had feared. They found the judge and the defense attorney to be less threatening than they had anticipated. These findings should be considered, however, in light of the strong likelihood that the children who were most upset by the experience may have declined our postcourt interview. Thus, we probably missed interviewing some of the children who were most distressed by the experience.

Even though the experience of testifying was less aversive than initially feared by the children we interviewed, many children still found the event upsetting. One child told us that it was "worse than I thought—like a nightmare." Another stated, "[I felt] scared, really upset, and I just couldn't remember that many things." And, even though the defense attorneys' popularity improved, they were still unpopular. One teenager commented, for example, "I can't stand him. He made me mad. He kept trying to, he'd say, 'Didn't you say this?' and I didn't. He kept trying to make me lie." When the defense attorneys were judged more positively, these more positive judgments were accompanied by comments like, "He was nice. He didn't try to twist my words around like they do on People's Court. I was worried he might twist my words around." These comments indicate that at least some of the children fully understood that the defense attorney might try to discredit them.

The most striking finding concerned the children's negative attitudes toward facing the defendant. This is particularly important in light of the constitutional right to face-to-face confrontation and attempts to moderate that right in cases involving child victim/witnesses (*Maryland v. Craig*, 1990). The children generally did not state why facing the defendant was objectionable, but we gained some insights nevertheless. One reason concerned threats to the child and family. For example, one 5-year-old child ran to her mother after testifying and stated with relief that the defendant had not given her "the evil eye." She was relieved by this, she continued, because it meant that the defendant was not going to kill her, just her mother! (The defendant had allegedly threatened to kill both the mother and the child if the assault were reported.)

Fear of the defendant was a common response. A number of children stated that they were so frightened that they tried not to look at the defendant. One young adolescent said, "I was scared. I didn't look at him. If I would have looked at him, I would have freaked." Other children complained that seeing the defendant "brought the memory all back again." Instead of fear, some children expressed anger at seeing the defendant and/or the defendant's courtroom behavior. One child noted, "He was making me mad. He was acting it up for the jury, mouthing 'I can't believe you're doing this.'" Finally, some children expressed mixed emotions. These children tended to express the desire to see the defendant convicted but were frightened at the thought of testifying. One such child commented during the Before-Court Measure interview, "In some ways, I wish he was there so I can show him I'm going to put him in jail. In some ways I don't. He'll make me scared and give dirty looks." We conclude that, at least from the perspective of many of the children, negative feelings about testifying in front of the defendant lend support to recent innovative procedures, such as the use of closed-circuit television, that remove the child or the defendant from the courtroom.

IX. FAMILIES' EXPERIENCES OF THE LEGAL SYSTEM

The Legal Involvement Questionnaire was designed to tap children's and caretakers' reactions to legal participation. Regardless of the emotional effects of criminal court involvement, attitudes about the legal system are important because they are likely to affect children's and adults' subsequent willingness to report crime and become involved in prosecutions again. Such attitudes might also affect participants' perceptions of justice.

On the Legal Involvement Questionnaire, respondents were additionally asked to report their suggestions for changes in the way their cases were handled by the legal system. The children's and caretakers' answers provide valuable insights, from the victim's and family's point of view, about where improvements could be made.

At the time of the final follow-up, or, alternatively, as cases closed, we asked caretakers and children to complete our Legal Involvement Questionnaire. At the end of the study, we sent these questionnaires to the rest of the families whether or not their cases had closed. Separate questionnaires for adults and children were provided. As mentioned earlier (see Chap. III), the two questionnaires differed in the number and wording of questions, with the goal of making the children's form as concise, nonstressful, and understandable as possible. For example, adults were asked to rate the legal experience for themselves and then for their children, whereas children were asked to complete the questionnaire for themselves only.

These questionnaires—the last official forms completed by the participants—were returned by 73 children and 103 adults. An additional nine questionnaires provided by adults were discounted because the adults had not lived with the child for a considerable amount of time during the prosecution. Thus, about 50% of the adults returned the forms, but only 33% of the children did. The lower return rate by the children, which makes conclusions based on their responses especially tentative, can be explained by a number of factors, one being that some of the children were too young to complete the forms themselves. Also, a number of caretakers told us that they did not want their children to have to think about the case again and so did not give the form to them. The children who did respond ranged in age from 5 to 18 years ($M = 11.8$ years, SD = 3.38). Caretakers of young children were instructed that they could help their children complete the form if necessary.

Of the completed questionnaires that we received, 85 were from caretakers, and 57 were from children ($M = 11.97$ years, SD = 3.40) whose cases had closed. We report here only the findings for these respondents since they were in the best position to answer all the questions.

The children and adults were asked to indicate (as checks on our records) whether the child had testified and, if not, whether the child had appeared at the courthouse. They were also asked to rate the effects on the child of testifying or not testifying, the quality of their interactions with legal personnel, their satisfaction with the outcome of the case, the effect of the legal involvement on their lives, how fair the criminal justice process seemed, and their feelings about the speed of the proceedings. The adults were also asked to indicate the effects of legal involvement on various aspects of their own lives (e.g., marital relationship, work), how informed they had been kept about the case, and how many times their child had been questioned by authorities, not counting questioning in court. Finally, both children and adults were asked to describe any changes they would like to see in the legal process.

It should be noted that the analyses in this section compare "testifiers" ($N = 25$) with "nontestifiers" ($N = 32$), not testifiers with matched controls. This comparison allowed us to include a larger number of subjects. Despite the fact that the two groups were not officially matched, a series of independent two-tailed t tests confirmed that the two groups did not differ significantly on our matching variables.

In terms of mean responses, children rated their satisfaction with the case outcome as being "somewhat satisfied," $M = 2.85$, SD = 1.20, and the fairness of the legal system as being "somewhat fair," $M = 1.92$, SD = .98. Their ratings of the effect of legal participation on their lives and of the speed of the legal system both fell between "somewhat bad" and "somewhat good," $M = 2.61$, SD = .98, and $M = 2.71$, SD = 1.04, respectively, and thus were more negative. These means are partially deceiving, however, in that they hide distinct subgroups of children who fell at the ends of the distributions. For example, 22 children indicated that they were "very satisfied" with the outcome of the case, but 12 indicated that they were "very unsatisfied" with it. Eight children indicated that legal involvement had a "very good" effect on their lives, whereas 10 indicated that it had a "very bad" effect. Of the testifiers, only two indicated that it had a "very good" effect on their lives, whereas four indicated that it had a "very bad" effect.

This variability in the children's reports may in part be the source of professionals' beliefs that legal involvement is traumatic for some children but cathartic for others.

On these same variables, the caretakers' ratings were similar to the children's except that the adults were slightly more negative, with their mean scores tending to fall between "somewhat negative" and "somewhat positive": satisfaction with outcome of the case, $M = 2.45$, SD $= 1.17$; fairness of legal system, $M = 2.42$, SD $= 1.06$; effect of legal participation on their children's lives, $M = 2.61$, SD $= 0.81$; effect of legal participation on their own lives, $M = 2.54$, SD $= 0.95$; and speed of the legal system, $M = 2.89$, SD $= 1.02$. Again, these means mask wide variability in the responses on many of the measures. For the adults, almost as many indicated that legal involvement had a very negative as indicated that it had a very positive effect on their lives (11 vs. 16), whereas, for their children, only five caretakers indicated that it had a very positive effect, and 11 indicated that it had a very negative effect. In terms of the adults' satisfaction with the outcome of the case, the scores were fairly evenly distributed across the four points of the scale, but the modal response was "very negative."

Comparisons between the testifiers' and the nontestifiers' responses and between the responses of their respective caretakers are presented in Tables 20 and 21. All t tests are two-tailed except for the "child's behavior worse" item, for which specific directional predictions were made. As can be seen

TABLE 20

Contrasts in Mean Ratings of Responses Given by Testifiers versus Nontestifiers and Their Parents on the Legal Involvement Questionnaire
(Closed Cases Only)

	Testifiers		Non-testifiers				
	M	(SD)	M	(SD)	t	df	p
Children:							
Effect of testifying/not testifying	2.17	(.96)	1.72	(.92)	1.76	54	.10
Satisfaction with case outcome	2.78	(1.20)	2.90	(1.21)	.35	51	...
Effect on child's life of legal involvement	2.57	(1.04)	2.64	(.95)	.28	49	...
Fairness of the legal system	1.80	(.75)	2.00	(1.11)	.68	49	...
Speed of the legal system	2.60	(1.10)	2.86	(.94)	.91	50	...
Parents:							
Effect of testifying/not testifying	2.40	(.97)	1.71	(.90)	3.26	79	.01
Parent satisfaction with case outcome	2.47	(1.22)	2.44	(1.15)	.09	80	...
Child satisfaction with case outcome	2.50	(1.14)	2.80	(1.24)	.99	67	...
Effect on parent's life of legal involvement	2.83	(1.05)	2.38	(.86)	2.14	81	.05
Effect on child's life of legal involvement	2.82	(.77)	2.49	(.82)	1.74	75	.10
Fairness of the legal system	2.55	(1.02)	2.34	(1.08)	.86	77	...
Speed of the legal system	3.00	(1.05)	2.83	(1.01)	.72	82	...
Communication about the case	2.23	(1.10)	2.29	(.92)	.28	83	...
Number of times child was questioned	5.43	(2.85)	5.17	(5.42)	.23	68	...

Note.—N equals $df - 2$.

TABLE 21

Contrasts in Percentages of Parents Responding Yes to "Has Involvement in the Criminal Prosecution of This Case Affected Your Life in Any of the Following Areas?" (Closed Cases Only)

	Parents of Testifiers	Parents of Nontestifiers	t	p
Marriage:				
Improved..........	13	4	1.68	.10
More problems	10	18	1.00	. . .
Work:				
Missed time........	43	38	.40	. . .
Worked extra	0	11	1.89	.10
Income:				
Loss	10	18	1.00	. . .
Increased..........	0	0	.00	. . .
Family:				
Closer.............	47	49	.21	. . .
More arguments....	37	35	.19	. . .
Child's behavior:				
Better.............	20	18	.20	. . .
Worse.............	47	29	1.63	.05
Faith in God:				
Increased..........	37	25	1.08	. . .
Decreased	5	5	.44	. . .
Friendships:				
Strained	33	24	.16	. . .
Strengthened.......	23	16	.78	. . .
Social contact:				
Increased..........	30	11	2.25	.05
Decreased	23	31	.74	. . .

Note.—All t tests are two tailed except for "child's behavior: worse"; $df = 83$ for all items. $N = df - 2$.

in Table 20, adults and children rated the effects of not testifying as more positive than the effects of testifying. For this comparison, when the child did not testify, both the child and the adult rated the effects on the child of not testifying, whereas when the child did testify, the child and the adult rated the effect on the child of testifying. The comparison was significant for adults and approached significance for children.

Few of the other means significantly differed as a function of whether the children testified. One that did concerned the effect of legal involvement on the caretakers' lives. Caretakers of children who testified indicated that participation in the criminal investigation and prosecution had a more adverse effect on their lives than did caretakers whose children did not testify. The same question asked of the caretakers regarding the effect of criminal investigation and prosecution on their children's lives was only marginally significant.

No significant differences in ratings of their interactions with legal staff (e.g., police, defense attorney, judge) obtained between caretakers of testifiers and nontestifiers. Except for ratings of defense attorneys, $M = 2.64$, $SD = 1.10$, all mean ratings ranged between 1.1 ("very positive") and 1.9 ("somewhat positive") on the four-point scale. Children who testified gave significantly more positive ratings to VAs, $M = 1.23$, $SD = 0.69$, and prosecutors, $M = 1.21$, $SD = 0.42$, than those who did not, $M = 1.71$, $SD = 0.85$, and $M = 1.67$, $SD = 0.82$, respectively. Otherwise, the pattern of both groups' ratings paralleled that of their caretakers. Thus, children who testified were more satisfied than children who did not with the performance of the prosecutor and the VA. Of course, children who testified had greater exposure to these legal professionals and to their helping role. It should be noted that, in general, children and caretakers had positive feelings toward all the legal personnel. The most negative ratings were for the defense attorneys, but even they were not rated extremely negatively.

Another significant difference was that caretakers of children who testified compared to caretakers of children who did not were more likely to report an increase in social contacts (see Table 21). Perhaps the testifiers' greater involvement in the legal system brought some of the more isolated families into contact with others (e.g., the attorneys, social workers) or prompted caretakers to join with family members and friends for emotional support. Surprisingly, there was a trend for improvement in marital happiness to be associated with children's testifying. Although this effect was only marginally significant, it suggests that, in general, testifying did not have a negative effect on spousal relations.

The number of caretakers who reported improvement in the children's behavior was low, and the number did not differ for caretakers of testifiers and caretakers of nontestifiers. However, caretakers of testifiers were more likely than caretakers of nontestifiers to indicate that, as a result of the criminal prosecution, their children's behavior worsened. As seen earlier, when this variable was compared for the matched cases, the findings also indicated that the caretakers of testifiers were more likely to indicate that their children's adjustment worsened than were caretakers of control children.

Predicting testifiers' and nontestifiers' reactions.—We next examined correlates of the children's and caretakers' responses. Table 22 presents significant correlations for the children who testified and the children who did not. As can be seen, only three variables predicted the testifiers' attitudes about testifying: children who experienced more severe abuse, who lacked maternal support, or who looked more frightened of the defendant in court indicated that the effects of testifying were more negative than did children who experienced less severe abuse, enjoyed maternal support, or looked less frightened of the defendant. In addition, the caretaker's social adjustment score was associated with how the caretaker perceived the effect of testifying on the child: more poorly adjusted caretakers believed that the

TABLE 22

CORRELATIONS INDICATING PREDICTOR VARIABLES FOR CHILDREN'S AND PARENTS'
RESPONSES CONCERNING THE EFFECTS OF TESTIFYING OR NOT TESTIFYING
(Closed Cases Only)

	CHILDREN		PARENTS	
	Testifying, r	Not Testifying, r	Testifying, r	Not Testifying, r
Severity	.48*	.05	.11	.07
	(N = 24)	(N = 32)	(N = 30)	(N = 51)
Guilty outcome.	−.22	−.57**	−.02	−.54**
	(N = 14)	(N = 31)	(N = 29)	(N = 50)
Previous abuse	.00	.62**	−.34	.43**
	(N = 16)	(N = 21)	(N = 20)	(N = 34)
Felt responsible	.11	.55**	−.01	.33*
	(N = 17)	(N = 22)	(N = 21)	(N = 42)
Maternal support. . .	−.51*	.29	−.17	.25
	(N = 23)	(N = 27)	(N = 29)	(N = 46)
SAS	.05	.32*	−.37*	.39**
	(N = 24)	(N = 31)	(N = 30)	(N = 50)
Looked frightened of defendant.	.58*	. . .	−.17	. . .
	(N = 15)		(N = 18)	

NOTE.—For nontestifiers, correlations are not possible for "looked frightened of defendant."
* $p < .05$.
** $p < .01$.

children were not as badly affected by testifying as did better-adjusted caretakers. (The mean social adjustment scores for the caretakers as a whole and for the caretakers of testifiers were 1.49, SD = 0.55, N = 214, and 1.57, SD = 0.55, N = 42, respectively, scores that compare favorably with that of a community sample, M = 1.59, as reported by Weissman et al., 1978.)

As indicated in Table 23, a number of the variables were intercorrelated. Of the four variables significantly related to the effects on children of testifying, only severity and maternal support were significantly related. (Children who had suffered more severe abuse received less maternal support at the time of disclosure.) When abuse severity was controlled, the correlation between the effects of testifying and maternal support was substantial but no longer significant, $r = -.33, N = 13$. Similarly, when maternal support was controlled, the correlation between the effects of testifying and severity was again substantial but no longer significant, $r = .39, N = 14$. This pattern suggests that some combination of abuse severity and lack of maternal support—but perhaps not either variable alone—led children to feel that the effects of testifying were negative.

The results are consistent with the findings for the court observations that fear of testifying in front of the defendant and abuse severity influence

TABLE 23

INTERCORRELATIONS BETWEEN PREDICTOR VARIABLES OF CHILDREN'S AND PARENTS' RESPONSES TO LEGAL INVOLVEMENT QUESTIONS
CONCERNING THE EFFECTS OF TESTIFYING OR NOT TESTIFYING (Closed Cases Only)

	2	3	4	5	6	7
1. Severity	.64** (N = 17)	.18* (N = 118)	.33** (N = 119)	-.25** (N = 148)	-.03 (N = 165)	.18 (N = 21)
2. Not guilty outcome		-.58* (N = 10)	.17 (N = 10)	-.29 (N = 16)	.19 (N = 17)	.28 (N = 7)
3. Previous abuse			.23* (N = 87)	-.28** (N = 108)	-.18* (N = 118)	.00 (N = 14)
4. Felt responsible				.04 (N = 109)	-.02 (N = 117)	.50* (N = 15)
5. Maternal support					-.02 (N = 148)	-.08 (N = 20)
6. SAS						.08 (N = 21)
7. Looked frightened of defendant						

* $p < .05$.
** $p < .01$.

children's reactions to testifying in criminal court. They are also consistent with the finding that maternal support influences testifiers' well-being.

A number of factors were also associated with how the nontestifiers felt about not testifying. When the case outcome was "not guilty," either through a plea bargain or through a court decision, children who did not testify felt worse about not testifying. Children who had physical abuse experiences prior to the incidents at issue in the current legal case or who felt more responsibility for their abuse were more likely to rate the effects of not testifying as negative. Children whose caretakers were more disturbed were more unhappy that they did not testify than children whose caretakers were less disturbed. Caretakers confirmed their children's feelings. Apparently, these children were more likely to want to have their voices heard. When the outcome was "not guilty," nontestifiers probably felt that their testimony might have swayed the trier of fact (judge or jury) toward a guilty verdict. For children who had previously experienced abuse, testifying might have been viewed as compensating for past resentment about not being heard. Alternatively, perhaps these children were simply more accustomed to legal participation. Children who felt some responsibility for the abuse may have thought that testifying would help them shed responsibility by publicly sharing it. In addition, caretakers whose social adjustment was low, as indicated by the SAS, rated the effects on their children of not testifying as worse.

Table 23 shows that some of the predictors of negative effects of not testifying were correlated with each other. Previous abuse was correlated significantly with feeling responsible and with the caretaker's low social adjustment, although these two variables were not correlated with each other. The correlations (one for children's reports and one for caretakers' reports) between previous abuse and feeling that the effects of not testifying were negative were recomputed with feeling responsible and parent's SAS partialed. The correlations actually went up: $r = .76$, $p < .001$, for the children's reports; $r = .54$, $p < .01$, for the caretakers' reports. The correlations for children and caretakers between feeling responsible and feeling that the effects of not testifying were negative were recomputed, partialing out previous abuse. The correlations for children and caretakers were essentially unchanged, .54 and .29, although the latter fell below the .05 level. Finally, the correlation between SAS and the child's feeling that the effects of not testifying were negative was recomputed with previous abuse partialed. Both correlations increased: $r = .56$, $p = .01$, for the children's reports; $r = .53$, $p < .01$, for the caretakers' reports. Taken together, these results indicate that the significant relations shown in Table 22 can be interpreted individually. All but one remain large and significant even when potentially confounded variables are partialed.

The results indicate, then, that children have negative feelings about not testifying if the case results in a not guilty outcome or if the children were previously abused, feel responsible for being abused, or have a care-taker who exhibits relatively poor social adjustment.

Several items on the measures we collected when the children were at the courthouse were associated with their later attitudes and with their caretakers' reports as well. In general, the more negative or upset the children were about testifying, the more negative were their later attitudes about legal participation. Children who were more negative about testifying in court as reflected on our After-Court Measure and who had higher scores on the Day-of-Court Measure concerning internalizing problems (e.g., fear-fulness, trouble sleeping) rated legal involvement as more negative, $r = .61$, $N = 14$, $p < .02$, and $r = .40$, $N = 28$, $p < .05$, respectively. Similarly, the more negative the child felt about testifying immediately after having done so, the more likely the caretaker was to indicate that the effect of legal participation on the child was negative, $r = .53$, $N = 17$, $p < .05$. Children whose mood was sadder while they testified later rated the system as less fair, $r = .59$, $N = 15$, $p < .05$, and the worse the child felt about testifying in front of the defendant, the more likely the caretaker was to report that the child was unsatisfied with the outcome of the case, $r = -.52$, $N = 15$, $p < .05$. Thus, children's feelings about testifying were associated with later negative attitudes toward the legal system. It is possible, however, that these results are at least in part a product of some children who were simply more negative generally or of caretakers whose negative attitudes about the legal system influenced their children's attitudes.

Predicting children's and caretaker's reactions generally.—Correlations were also calculated with the testifiers and the nontestifiers combined. There were no significant correlations between the children's responses to items on our Legal Involvement Questionnaire and their age or relationship to the defendant. However, three child factors were significantly related to the children's attitudes. The more severe the abuse, $r = .41$, $N = 51$, $p < .01$, and the longer the abuse lasted, $r = .32$, $N = 52$, $p < .025$, the more negatively the child rated the effect of the legal system on her or his life. Also, children's gender was predictive of how satisfied children were with the outcome of the case, with females being less satisfied than males, $r = .37$, $N = 53$, $p < .01$.

Concerning family-system factors, the amount of support that children received at home was significantly related to children's feelings about the legal system. If another child in the same household was a victim, children rated the effect of legal involvement on their lives as being less negative, $r = -.42$, $N = 49$, $p < .01$. Children also rated the effects of legal involve-ment on their lives as less negative if they had maternal support, $r = -.29$, $N = 47$, $p < .05$. Thus, children who felt support at home, either by virtue of having a sibling who was also a victim or by virtue of having a mother who was supportive, were less likely to find legal involvement aversive than children who had less support at home, again indicating the important role of family-system factors.

The family's socioeconomic standing was associated with the caretakers' responses: caretakers of children in lower-income families were more likely to report that the effect of court involvement on the child's life was negative than were higher-income families, $r = .23$, $N = 76$, $p < .01$.

Several legal-system factors were also related to the children's and families' responses to items on our Legal Involvement Questionnaire. Consistent with the findings of Tedesco and Schnell (1987), children who experienced more interviews by police and other authorities before the court hearings rated their legal involvement more negatively, $r = .41$, $N = 38$, $p < .05$. This finding is interesting in light of the results reported above for the children's CBCL scores: as will be recalled, the number of interviews was not associated with the children's improvement. Thus, although the number of interviews did not predict whether the children's general well-being improved, it was associated with their attitudes toward legal involvement, an important consideration in its own right.

However, the most pervasive legal factor associated with the children's and caretakers' responses was case outcome. Although as indicated above a gender difference emerged in satisfaction with the case outcome, in general the children's and caretakers' attitudes toward the legal system were strongly associated with case outcome, regardless of gender. Using the guilty (plea bargain or "guilty" trial outcome) versus not-guilty (dismissal or "not guilty"/ hung jury trial outcome) variable, a not-guilty outcome was associated with more negative ratings by the children concerning the fairness of the legal system, $r = -.35$, $N = 45$, $p < .025$. When a guilty verdict was reached, caretakers also rated the system as more fair, $r = -.34$, $N = 72$, $p < .01$, and the effect of legal involvement on their lives as more positive, $r = -.24$, $N = 75$, $p < .05$. Not surprisingly, caretakers rated their own and their child's satisfaction with the outcome of the case as more positive if the defendant was found guilty at trial, $r = .84$, $N = 76$, $p < .001$, and $r = .79$, $N = 76$, $p < .01$, respectively, or if there was a guilty outcome in general, $r = .44$, $N = 76$, $p < .001$, and $r = .44$, $N = 76$, $p < .001$, respectively. Thus, understandably, the families felt more satisfied and that the system was more fair if the defendant was convicted.

Again implicating the importance of the interaction of family and legal systems, the caretakers' social adjustment was significantly related to attitudes about case outcome. Specifically, caretakers' social adjustment predicted their report of how satisfied the child was with the case outcome: the more disturbed caretakers indicated that their children were less satisfied with the case outcome, $r = -.27$, $N = 52$, $p < .05$. This finding does not simply reflect adult bias since children of more disturbed caretakers also reported greater dissatisfaction with case outcome, $r = -.29$, $N = 52$,

$p < .05$. Since caretaker disturbance did not in fact significantly predict whether the defendant was convicted, these findings suggest that caretaker disturbance affects children's attitudes about case outcome because such caretakers do not help their children accept the case's final disposition.

SUGGESTED CHANGES

What features of the legal system would the families like to see changed? In exploring answers to this question, we again considered statements from all the respondents, not just the testifiers and the control families. Eighty-three percent of the caretakers who returned questionnaires responded to this question. (Because caretakers at times mentioned multiple changes, the percentages presented below add to more than 100.) A common response, given by 37% of the adult respondents, was that the legal process should move more quickly. Also common was the suggestion that alternative means for taking the child's testimony should be instituted (39%), such as the admission of videotaped testimony, the elimination of cross-examination of child witnesses, or the use of professionals to testify for the child. (The latter procedure is commonly used in some countries, such as Israel; see David, 1990; and Harnon, 1990.) Caretakers also commented that greater respect should be paid to the child victim's rights (23%) and that defendants should be given harsher sentences (23%). A number of caretakers mentioned that the child should not have to face the defendant (9%), a comment implicit in suggestions concerning videotaped testimony or professionals who would testify for the child. Only 6% of the caretakers indicated that the legal system was fine the way it was. Thus, 94% of the caretakers who answered this question wanted to see changes.

Sixty-nine percent of the children who returned questionnaires responded to our open-ended question. Nineteen percent of those who did commented on the need to shorten the length of their legal involvement. Twenty-one percent mentioned that alternative means for taking their testimony should have been used, such as videotaped testimony, limits on the types of questions that could be asked, or not having the defendant present in the courtroom. Twenty-six percent indicated that no changes in the system were needed, but 74% indicated that changes should be made.

SUMMARY

Attitudes about the legal system are important for understanding the effects of legal participation on children. Our findings indicate that, on average, the effects of not testifying are viewed as more positive than the effects of testifying.

Our findings also indicate that different factors predict testifiers' reactions to testifying and nontestifiers' reactions to not testifying. Children who were visibly frightened of testifying in front of the defendant and who had been severely abused and/or who lacked maternal support were more likely to feel that testifying had a negative effect on them. In contrast, children who did not testify regretted not testifying if the defendant was found not guilty, if they felt in some way responsible for the abuse, if they had a poorly adjusted caretaker, or if they had endured past abuse.

The children and families had a number of suggestions for changes in the legal system. These suggestions were aimed primarily at making the experience of testifying less stressful for the children.

X. DISCUSSION

This study indicates that testifying in criminal court, at least as the system is traditionally constituted, is associated with negative effects for many, but not all, child sexual assault victims. The negative effects are more evident in the short than the long term. But negative effects, particularly in a subgroup of children, are still present even after the prosecution ends. Our findings confirm those of previous researchers (DeFrancis, 1969; Gibbens & Prince, 1963; Oates & Tong, 1987; Runyan et al., 1988; Tedesco & Schnell, 1987) but also offer new insights into children's fears, experiences, performance, and attitudes associated with legal involvement.

Our findings are also surprisingly consistent with studies of children's reactions to other stressful events, such as hospitalization and divorce. For example, in regard to several of these situations, multiple exposures to a stressor and lack of parental support are known to exacerbate children's distress, as was uncovered in the present investigation as well. Moreover, in our study, as in research on children's reactions to anxiety-provoking events generally, vulnerability and protective factors associated with the systems of the child and the family and with the specific stressful event (in the present case, testifying in criminal court) were identified. Below, we summarize our main findings and discuss their implications.

BEHAVIORAL ADJUSTMENT AND ATTITUDES TOWARD LEGAL INVOLVEMENT

The main goal of the present study was to determine whether testifying in criminal court is deleterious or beneficial for children. On average, the short-term effects on the children's behavioral adjustment, as reported by their caretakers, were more harmful than helpful. In contrast, by the time the cases were resolved, the behavioral adjustment of most, but not all, children who testified was similar to that of children who did not take the stand. The general course for these children, as for the control children, was gradual improvement. Nevertheless, continued involvement as a witness for the prosecution can at least temporarily interfere with children's adjustment.

In considering the extent of the children's reactions, it is informative to compare the children's CBCL scores to Achenbach and Edelbrock's (1983) norms. On average, the children in our study scored within the clinical range at intake, especially on the total and internalizing T scales. Scores of children who testified continued to fall within the clinical range or hovered closely around the clinical cutoff at the three follow-up assessments, whereas the control children's scores tended to fall in the normal range by the time of the 7-month and final follow-up tests. Of note, total T scores for the subset of children who did not improve, as assessed at the 7-month and final follow-ups, rose from about 63 (the clinical cutoff) to over 70. These findings indicate that, at the start of the prosecution, the children's well-being was already precarious; the legal system, along with the child and family systems, then played a role in exacerbating or lessening these vulnerable children's disturbance. Given that the legal system is likely to be dealing with many child victim/witnesses who evince clinical disturbance or who are just on the border of the clinical range, sensitivity by the legal system to their needs seems justified.

How do the child, family, and legal systems, and the interaction among these three systems, influence children's behavioral adjustment to and attitudes about criminal court involvement? We turn next to a discussion of our results concerning child-, family-, and legal-system factors and relate our findings to earlier research on children's reactions to the legal system and stressful events generally. We also identify subgroups of children who may profit from special consideration by the courts.

The child system.—Although we expected age differences in children's reactions to criminal court involvement, surprisingly few appeared in the children's behavioral adjustment, as reported by their caretakers. One might predict that younger children would be less stressed by legal involvement because they would have less understanding of the implications of their testimony for their own or the defendant's life. Conversely, younger children might be more stressed by testifying since they would be more intimidated, confused, and emotionally vulnerable. In fact, it was only at the first follow-up that age differences emerged in behavioral disturbance. Older and younger children, compared to 6–11-year-olds, showed less improvement as evinced in the children's total and externalizing behavioral problems scores. This pattern is consistent with the possibility that younger children are stressed because of their vulnerability whereas older children are stressed because of their greater awareness. Because these findings did not replicate at the 7-month and final follow-ups, and because initial (pretestimony) differences in behavioral disturbance existed for one age group at the 3-month follow-up, caution is needed in interpreting these results.

Studies of children's coping indicate that the relation between age and reactions to stressful events is not a simple one. Consistent with conclusions regarding children's reactions to stressful events such as divorce and birth of a sibling (Dunn, 1988; Rutter, 1983), it may be the form rather than the extent of children's reactions to testifying that is influenced by age; that is, children of all ages may have adverse reactions but express those reactions in somewhat different ways. Future studies using more sensitive measures may uncover more definitive age relations in behavioral disturbance associated with testifying in court.

Although consistent age differences failed to emerge when caretaker ratings of adjustment were considered, when asked directly about testifying, either before entering the courtroom or emerging from it, older children expressed more negative feelings than younger children. There are several possible reasons for the older children's more negative attitudes. Older children's greater understanding of the legal system (e.g., Saywitz, 1989), with concomitant increases in the ability to predict aversive courtroom experiences and to appreciate the significance of legal outcomes, might underlie their more negative attitudes. Moreover, older children's awareness of taboos concerning sexuality may result in greater embarrassment over having to discuss sexual activity in public (Goldman & Goldman, 1982; Saywitz, Goodman, Nichols, & Moan, 1991). It is also possible that part of the older children's negativity resulted from developmental issues: during adolescence, self-determination and autonomy become increasingly important. Given the lack of control that child victims may experience in the court system, adolescents may be particularly at risk of experiencing the process as coercive (see Hetherington et al., 1992).

In addition to age differences, gender differences emerged in the children's reports of their reactions to testifying; females expressed greater negativity about testifying in front of the defendant than did males. It is possible that females find the adversarial system, which is confrontational in nature, less to their liking and more foreign to their experiences than do males (Gilligan, 1982). Alternatively, females may be more willing than males to express negative and fearful emotions. In any case, the gender difference is worthy of note because the majority of children involved in child sexual abuse prosecutions are female.

The family system.—Features of the family system were also important in influencing the children's emotional reactions to testifying. In particular, maternal support was associated with improvement, whereas lack of support was associated with continued distress. Maternal support has been implicated as important for the emotional recovery of child sexual assault victims

(Conte & Berliner, 1988; Conte & Schuerman, 1987), and it has long been suspected to affect children's reactions to legal involvement. The role of maternal support as a protective factor in coping with the stress of legal involvement is consistent with the literature on the buffering effects of maternal and social support generally (e.g., Dunn, 1988; Gore, 1985; Musick, Stott, Spencer, Goldman, & Cohler, 1987; Rutter, 1983). Our findings establish that, when mothers react to the disclosure of abuse with hostility, distance, or preoccupation with others' needs (i.e., not the child's needs), their children have more difficulty dealing with the additional stress of legal involvement. This finding emerged from the analyses of the CBCL data as well as from the children's own reports, as obtained on our Legal Involvement Questionnaire. On the latter, children who lacked maternal support rated the effects of testifying and of legal involvement on their lives as being more negative than did children who enjoyed maternal support. A lack of maternal support was associated with the presence of a concurrent dependency and neglect case and with the child having a closer relationship to the defendant. This combination of factors points to a subgroup of children—specifically, incest victims—as being particularly at risk of traumatic effects of testifying, although any child who lacks maternal support should probably be considered at risk.

The legal system.—A set of stressors posed by the legal system itself was identified, some of which had a more or less pervasive effect on the children and some of which interacted with the child and family system to affect the children's reactions. The finding that testifying multiple times was associated with continued distress is consistent with the results of several previous studies. Tedesco and Schnell (1987) found that victims reported that legal involvement was less helpful the more often they had to testify. DeFrancis (1969) and Gibbens and Prince (1963) also reported that testifying is associated with distress in child sexual assault victims. Our findings indicate, however, that testifying once does not, on average, lead to increased behavioral disturbance, at least as reported by parents, whereas multiple testimony experiences do. The findings are also consonant with those reported in studies of young children's reactions to hospitalization; one hospital admission is not associated with long-term disturbance, but multiple exposures are (Rutter, 1983). It is possible that children can cope with one exposure to a stressful event but that multiple exposures start to erode children's resilience and have a sensitizing effect.

According to the framework developed in this *Monograph*, a child's experience in court is partly determined by the courts' response to a unique set of characteristics and resources of the child and family systems. As mentioned earlier, it may be possible then to identify subgroups of children who are at particular risk for lack of improvement related to their court involvement. In the present study, testifying more than once was the variable most highly associated with lack of improvement. Compared to children who testified only once, children who testified two or more times had higher CBCL scores at intake, had more traumas in their lives, and had higher Day-of-Court scores, indicating greater disturbance at intake as well as 48 hours before having to appear in court. They were rated as being more credible witnesses, and corroborative evidence was more likely to be associated with their claims. These children may have been more likely to testify because prosecutors perceived them as more credible witnesses—for example, if they were able to tell what happened believably, with corroborative evidence to back up their claims. However, these children may be particularly vulnerable. They were already exhibiting a high level of distress and may lack resources to handle more. In short, how professionals in the legal system select children for repeated legal involvement may in part be a function of characteristics of the child and family systems as well as of such legally relevant factors as the severity of the crime and the dangerousness of the accused. However, to the extent that the children selected for participation are particularly vulnerable, special consideration may need to be given to their welfare. Further reseach is needed to confirm this pattern, but, if replicable, the findings may provide a guide for intervention.

Another factor that is particularly important within the context of the legal system is the presence or absence of corroborative evidence. The absence of corroborating evidence was related to distress at the 7-month follow-up. Presumably, when corroborating testimony is lacking, greater emphasis is placed on the children's testimony and credibility. Adult rape victims as well as child sexual abuse victims have noted the particular stress associated with being the sole witness to their assaults and the resultant fear of not being believed (Brownmiller, 1975; Rush, 1980). Lack of corroboration is likely to be a source of concern not only for the child but also for those in decision-making roles (Leippe & Romancyzk, 1987).

The legal-system variables that we identified were particularly evident at the 7-month follow-up. Although by the time of the final follow-up a subset of children still had not improved, it was difficult to establish why. Contrary to our prediction, the more times the case was continued, the more likely the child's behavioral adjustment was to improve. This is surprising because it is commonly believed that continuances increase children's distress. Our finding appears to reflect the mere passage of time, however. Since continuances typically prolonged the case, continuances gave the children more time to recover. When the length of the legal process was controlled, the number of continuances experienced no longer predicted improvement. In cases where continuances are positively correlated with testifying multiple times, the effects of continuances might be confused with the effects of testifying. That is, although the continuances in themselves may not be harmful, they could lead to greater distress if they involve the child testifying multiple times. There were too few cases of this kind of continuance to determine the effects of this potentially important variable. Future research, ideally with a larger number of children, is needed to investigate this possibility.

Even though continuances gave children longer to improve, parents and children complained that the legal system moved too slowly. Thus, self-report measures pointed to length of legal involvement as a significant stressor. Such findings are consistent with former research indicating that prolonged involvement with criminal prosecution is distressing for children (e.g., Runyan et al., 1988).

In addition, other legal-system factors appeared to be predictive of the children's improvement. Parents who complained that the system was unfair, that they were unsatisfied with it, and/or that it had a negative effect on their children's or their own lives were more likely to have children who did not improve. The direction of these effects is unclear, however. On the one hand, it would be understandable for parents of children who do not improve to be more unhappy with the legal system; perhaps in such cases the legal system was more unfair and more destructive for the children. On the other hand, since parents filled out both the CBCL and the Legal Involvement Questionnaire, it is possible that parents who were more unhappy with the legal system projected their feelings onto their child's behavior or were just more likely to report negative feelings generally, seeing both their children and the legal system in a negative light.

That certain legal-system factors (e.g., case outcome) did not predict improvement as measured by the CBCL was as interesting as the fact that others did. One might also expect certain child-system factors (e.g., gender, severity of the abuse suffered) and family-system factors (e.g., SES) to be related to improvement in behavioral adjustment, but they were not. Some of these factors might have emerged as significant predictors if a larger number of cases had been available for study. Also, although some of these factors were not associated with adjustment as measured by the CBCL, they were related to the children's and parents' attitudes about legal involvement once the cases closed.

Regarding these attitudes, there were again clear subgroups of children and parents who found legal participation to be more upsetting, again reflecting the influence of legal-system factors often in combination with child- and family-system factors: more severely abused children, females, children who had less family support, children whose parents evinced low social adjustment, children from poorer families, children who experienced repeated interviewing by authorities, and children who, on the day of court, were more fearful of the defendant and more negative about testifying. Based on research concerning children's reactions to stressful events, many of the factors associated with children's later attitudes would be expected to place the children at risk. For example, compared to less severely abused children, those who suffered more severe abuse would, because of their former trauma, be expected to be especially at risk when confronted with a stressful event that provides links to the former trauma.

One such link that is of considerable importance legally is facing the defendant, which emerged repeatedly in the study as an important legal-system factor associated with children's attitudes about testifying. In a very real sense, facing the defendant reexposes the child to part of the original precourt stressor, that is, the assault. Although only young children may fail to realize that the defendant cannot hurt them in the courtroom, regardless of age, seeing the defendant again may revive traumatic memories, reawakening feelings of anger, hurt, and helplessness. However, it is worthy of note that such feelings may occur in or out of the courtroom. One mother wrote to us after our study ended, saying that she felt that her child was not traumatized by the legal process but that events after the case closed were much worse. The defendant, who was on probation, moved back into his home across the street from the child, and the child lived in fear that she would be assaulted again. Despite the financial burden, the family eventually had to move to a new neighborhood, further disrupting the child's life. Unfortunately, such fears are not entirely unjustified: in a recent case in California, a man raped a girl when she was 9, threatening that he would attack her a second time when she was older. Six years later, after he was let out on parole without the family being notified, he kidnapped and raped the girl again ("Alleged Rape Victim Sues over Parole," 1991). Such distressing examples indicate that it is also important to study child victims' experiences, reactions, and attitudes well after the cases have closed.

Children's attitudes about legal involvement, such as facing the defendant or the fairness of the legal system, may in the long run be as important, if not more important, than their behavioral adjustment, especially if perturbations in the latter are relatively short lived. Even after behavioral symptoms associated with exposure to a stressful event subside, attitudes may prevail. If those attitudes are negative (e.g., that the system is unfair), children may be at risk of failing to report new experiences of victimization or developing pessimistic attitudes about justice generally. If the attitudes are positive (e.g., that fair treatment is possible), even though the event may have been anxiety provoking and disturbing at the time, it may be viewed as justifiable and worth the distress, and at least faith in the justness of the legal system is maintained. Thus, to obtain a complete understanding of children's reactions to legal involvement, studies are needed of both children's emotional reactions to and their attitudes about testifying—as well as of not testifying.

Regarding the latter, we were also able to identify a subgroup of children who were upset that they did not have their day in court. Some children who did not testify—those who felt some responsibility for the abuse, those who had been victimized before, and those whose cases ended in a not-guilty outcome—later regretted their lack of legal participation. Although we concentrated mainly on the reactions of children who took the stand, it is also important to consider the effects on children of not being allowed to testify. These children may also be at risk of negative attitudes about legal involvement, and, in addition to feelings of lack of control resulting from their victimization, they might feel disempowered again by not being able to help convict the offender.

CHILDREN'S COURTROOM APPREHENSIONS, EXPERIENCES, AND EYEWITNESS TESTIMONY

Other goals of the present study were, on the day of court, to determine children's apprehensions about testifying, the nature of their courtroom experiences, and the characteristics of their eyewitness reports. Our pre- and postcourt measures were designed to tap children's feelings about testifying, having a nonoffending parent present, being questioned by the attorneys, talking to the judge, and seeing the defendant again. One of the most interesting findings was that, although children expressed considerable apprehension about testifying, they emerged from the courtroom feeling better about the experience than they had expected. In particular, they felt better about testifying, about the judge, and even about the defense attorney (although the defense attorney was still seen in a negative light). Some of the positivity expressed related to relief that the event was over. The children's feelings about testifying in front of the defendant did not change, however. They expressed very negative feelings about testifying in front of the defendant both before and after they entered the courtroom. These findings lend support to recent efforts to shield child witnesses from the defendant via closed-circuit television or videotaped testimony (e.g., *Maryland v. Craig*, 1990).

The courtroom observations of the children provide a firsthand account of their legal-system experiences. The children's age and the severity of the abuse seemed to have the greatest influence on their behavior and treatment. Older children could provide more detail, as could children involved in more severe cases, and older children were viewed as more credible witnesses, at least during the preliminary hearings. Children who appeared more anxious were also viewed as more credible. Also of interest is the finding that, the more frightened the child was of the defendant, the fewer of the prosecutors' questions the children could answer. With an occasional exception, the judges were quite passive in protecting the children.

The finding that older children could provide more detail is consistent with findings from laboratory studies of children's testimony (e.g., Goodman & Reed, 1986; Goodman, Rudy, Bottoms, & Aman, 1990; Leippe et al., 1991; Marin et al., 1979). Laboratory studies have also documented the effects of intimidation in inhibiting children's reports (e.g., Clarke-Stewart, Thompson, & Lepore, 1989; Dent, 1977; Peters, 1988; for a review, see Pipe & Goodman, 1991). The present research provides evidence for the generalizability of these laboratory findings to the courtroom. In contrast, findings from mock jury studies that younger compared to older child sexual assault victims are viewed as more credible witnesses (Duggan et al., 1989; Goodman et al., 1989) were not supported when ratings by our courtroom observers were considered. We do not know, however, how the actual jurors viewed the children's testimony. In any case, our findings suggest that mock jury studies should examine the influence of children's demeanor (e.g., anxiety) as well as age on perceived credibility.

Our hypotheses concerning family factors were not supported by our data: children who testified against a family member did not provide less detail or evince greater negativity about testifying when observed in the courtroom or when questioned about the experience. Predictions about innovative legal-system practices were supported, however. We had predicted that child victims/witnesses would evince less fear and provide more detail when granted social support and testimony aids, as offered by innovative courtroom procedures. Although few innovative techniques were used to help the children testify, those we could evaluate indicated that they were associated with less distress (e.g., crying) and more detail (e.g., being able to answer more questions). These findings are consistent with laboratory research indicating that the accuracy of children's testimony is increased by the provision of social support (Moston, 1987) and the use of props (Goodman & Aman, 1990). However, props were also associated with inconsistent testimony regarding peripheral details. Perhaps the props were somewhat distracting. We hope that future studies will determine the replicability and bases of our findings.

SATISFACTION AND SUGGESTIONS FOR CHANGE

How satisfied in the end were families with the legal system and legal involvement? As would be expected, the families were more satisfied if the defendant was found guilty. In any case, children and parents had a number of suggestions about how to make the experience less traumatic and more sastisfactory. Their suggestions included being able to testify on videotape, not having to testify in front of the defendant, elimination of cross-examination, and hastened legal involvement. Some of these changes would probably be interpreted as infringing on defendants' constitutional rights, however. This, of course, raises again the primary dilemma concerning children's testimony in criminal court: how to protect children from trauma while at the same time protecting defendants' rights. Our results indicate that families can do their part by supporting their children. Unfortunately, this is not a realistic option in many cases. The police can do their part by trying their best to obtain corroborating evidence whenever possible. The legal system can do its part by having the child testify fewer times and by shielding frightened children from the defendant, as needed. Perhaps use of alternative testimony procedures (e.g., videotapes) at preliminary hearings, when constitutional rights can be more broadly interpreted, would aid children. Also, children who are most at risk (e.g., those who have to testify multiple times, who lack maternal support, and whose claims are not supported by corroborating evidence) should be given special consideration by the courts. In addition to the more general literature on children's ability to cope with stressful events, our findings may provide guidelines to the legal system as to which children would most benefit from protective measures.

CAVEATS

A variety of caveats apply to our findings. Because we were working in a real-life legal setting, we could not manipulate and control variables as we would in the laboratory, and we could not randomly assign subjects to conditions. Studies embedded within a legal context invariably suffer from such difficulties. Here, we highlight some of the additional problems associated with our project.

One problem concerns the representativeness of our sample. Although a surprisingly high proportion of the people we approached agreed to participate, our sample was nonrepresentative in a number of ways. Families of incest victims, females, and older children were less likely to agree to participate than we had hoped. The resulting bias in our sample might have distorted our findings. Because children who failed to improve were ones who lacked maternal support, and because maternal support may be absent in a substantial proportion of incest cases (Everson et al., 1989), it is possible that our findings underestimate the negative effect of criminal court involvement on such children. Even for families who agreed to participate, we have missing data on a variety of measures, and the reasons for these omissions may have important implications for our findings. For example, children who refused to complete our After-Court Measure may have done so because they were too upset about their experiences in court to be interviewed. Thus, children who had the most negative experiences may have been unavailable for our postcourt interview, again biasing our findings toward a rosier picture of children's reactions to court involvement.

A second problem involves our heavy reliance on the CBCL, a single measure of children's disturbance that was completed by parents. Possible parental bias associated with our measure could have been examined and countered by observational measures, psychiatric interview, or self-report. Several considerations influenced our decision to use the CBCL as our main measure of the children's well-being. One concerned the difficulty of finding a valid and reliable measure of children's disturbance that was appropriate for a broad age range: the CBCL met our needs in this respect better than any other instrument; a good alternative was not apparent. Another concerned legal and ethical restrictions associated with the ongoing prosecutions. Because the children were involved in active criminal cases, prosecutors were hesitant for us to interview the children directly. If we had done so, defense attorneys might have claimed that we were tampering with the witnesses (as one attorney did when he saw a child completing our After-Court Measure). Moreover, defense attorneys might have been more likely to subpoena our data, potentially forcing us to violate researcher-participant confidentiality. Finally, even if prosecutors had approved direct interviews, our impression was that many parents would have declined participation in the study. As noted earlier, during our initial recruitment calls, parents often asked us if we had to interview their children and expressed concern that they were already enduring too many interviews by unfamiliar professionals.

The CBCL could also be criticized for not providing a sensitive measure of the types of problems that child sexual abuse victims evidence. Relatively few items on the CBCL deal with sexual problems, for example. Again, no better substitute was available. Fortunately, efforts to develop measures sensitive to emotional problems that result from child sexual abuse are currently under way (Friedrich et al., 1991).

Another problem concerns the relative paucity of subjects in relation to the many variables of interest. As a result, some of our findings may have been significant by chance alone. Statistical "purity" was further corrupted by the fact that it was impossible to obtain complete information on every child, resulting in missing data on a number of variables. These problems typically did not affect tests of our main hypotheses, however. Much of our study was admittedly exploratory, and future researchers should attempt to replicate or disconfirm our findings. Nevertheless, our main predictions concerning the effects of testifying were supported, and these findings stand on firmer statistical and conceptual ground.

Our findings might also be attacked on the basis that we studied only three jurisdictions, all in the same state. A nationwide study would be useful in determining whether some jurisdictions' procedures lead to less stressful outcomes for children. Fortunately, at least one such study is currently under way (Whitcomb & Runyan, 1992).

Finally, we followed the children for a relatively short time. We do not know how their legal experiences will affect them once they are older.

FUTURE DIRECTIONS

Much more research is needed before we will have a complete picture of the emotional effects of criminal court testimony on children. We would like to share with others several of our ideas for future research.

We did not study a number of potentially important contributions to children's reactions to court. For example, we did not evaluate the prosecutor's ability to establish rapport with the child and the family, and we had only sketchy data on the children's involvement with social services. Moreover, we had little information on the initial investigation phase by police and/or social services. Although our findings indicate that fear of the defendant was part of the stressful nature of testifying, other possible courtroom stressors (e.g., harshness of the questioning) could be examined in greater detail. Future researchers might profitably concentrate on these potentially informative areas.

Investigators should examine techniques to limit the emotional distress experienced by the subset of children most at risk for adverse effects of testifying. Although the Supreme Court recently ruled that closed-circuit television could be used to shield child witnesses in child sexual abuse cases, research is needed to determine if this technology is indeed beneficial. Also, it will be important to determine if its use unduly biases the jury toward guilt (see Swim, Borgida, & McCoy, 1991), as feared by some members of the Court (e.g., *Coy v. Iowa,* 1988). Preparation programs to aid children in coping with the stresses of testifying have recently been instituted and evaluated, showing promising results (Sas, 1991). Further research along these lines would be beneficial.

Our study concentrated mainly on children's reactions and somewhat on nonoffending parents' reactions to criminal court involvement. We did not interview defendants to obtain their side of the story. Research is just beginning to evaluate the perceptions and reactions of other participants (e.g., defense attorneys, judges, jurors) in child sexual abuse prosecutions (Gray, 1988; Tidwell & Lipovsky, 1991), perceptions that will help provide a more complete picture of legal involvement. Valuable lessons can be learned from such studies.

Most research on children's reactions to court involvement have concerned child sexual assault victims, probably because they are most likely to testify as victim/witnesses in American criminal courts (Leippe et al., 1989;

Whitcomb et al., 1985). Nevertheless, other children may also face distress when serving as witnesses. Reactions to legal involvement should also be studied in children who witness homicide (Pynoos & Eth, 1984), domestic violence (Goodman & Rosenberg, 1987), severe accidents (Terr, 1990), and other traumatic events.

Finally, future researchers interested in children's reactions to legal involvement would profit from exploring theoretical models developed to understand children's reactions to other stressful events (e.g., bereavement, divorce). It is possible that a more refined understanding of children's reactions to stressful events generally would result. For example, such models indicate that the meaning of the event to the child and changes in family interaction patterns that accompany stressful events have important influences on children's reactions (Dunn, 1988).

CONCLUSIONS

In conclusion, our findings confirm that testimony in criminal court is associated with adverse emotional effects for at least some children. Specifically, a subgroup of children who testify do not show as rapid or complete improvement as children who do not testify. Our findings can be interpreted in light of studies of children's reactions to other stressful events. Taken as a whole, these studies indicate that specific protective and vulnerability factors are operative, some specific to particular situations like the courtroom, but others more general in nature. Based on an understanding of these factors in relation to the child, family, and legal systems, it is possible that children in particular need of protection can be identified.

Although the findings of our study indicate that criminal court testimony is stressful for many children and often accompanied by dissatisfaction for children and caretakers, it need not be so. We did not study how the children were prepared for the ordeal of testifying, but our impression was that systematic attempts to prepare the children were made only infrequently. Once in court, few innovative techniques were used to make the event less burdensome. Under other circumstances, criminal court testimony may be less stressful (Berliner & Barbieri, 1984; Sas, 1991).

In any case, it would be incorrect to interpret our findings as supporting the view that child sexual abuse cases should not be prosecuted. We did not have a comparison group of nonprosecuted cases. Moreover, the distress of the subgroup of children who testified needs to be considered in light of the distress of the subgroup of children who were upset because they did not take the stand. Rather, our findings are more appropriately interpreted as indicating that changes in the current legal system are needed so that children can serve as more effective and less traumatized witnesses.

VARIABLES MENTIONED IN THIS REPORT

Sexual Assault Profile (adapted from Conte & Berliner, 1984)
    Date of first disclosure
    Date of disclosure to police or social services
    Date case filed at prosecutor's office
    Date of last offense
    Child's birth date
    Child's age (in years)
    Child's gender:
        1 (female) and 2 (male)
    Child's race/ethnicity:
        1 (majority) and 2 (minority)
    Age at onset of abuse (in years)
    Age at end of abuse (in years)
    Type of charges:
      First-, second-, or third-degree sexual assault:
        0 (no) and 1 (yes)
      Attempted rape:
        0 (no) and 1 (yes)
      Incest:
        0 (no) and 1 (yes)
      Sexual assault on a child:
        0 (no) and 1 (yes)
      Other offenses (charges involving child's body, such as kidnapping,
        child physical abuse):
        0 (no) and 1 (yes)
    Corroborative evidence (e.g., medical evidence, other witness):
        0 (no) and 1 (yes)
    Time lapse between last assault and victim report:
        1 (within 48 hours), 2 (2 days–2 weeks), 3 (2 weeks–1 month),
          4 (1 month–6 months), 5 (6 months or more)
    Frequency of sexually abusive contacts with the defendant:
        1 (one time), 2 (limited; 2–3 times), 3 (extended)

Previous sexual abuse:
  0 (no) and 1 (yes)
Previous physical abuse:
  0 (no) and 1 (yes)
Nonoffending parent was victim of sexual abuse:
  0 (no) and 1 (yes)
Maternal support at time of disclosure:
  0 (no: e.g., hostile, disbelief, concerned with self) and 1 (yes: e.g.,
    supportive)
Maternal support throughout legal process:
  0 (no: e.g., hostile, disbelief, concerned with self) and 1 (yes: e.g.,
    supportive)
Paternal support at time of disclosure:
  0 (no: e.g., hostile, disbelief, concerned with self) and 1 (yes: e.g.,
    supportive)
Paternal support throughout legal process:
  0 (no: e.g., hostile, disbelief, concerned with self) and 1 (yes: e.g.,
    supportive)
Child's perception of responsibility for the abuse:
  1 (no responsibility), 2 (partial responsibility), 3 (child blames self
    for abuse)
Child's belief about negative consequences:
  0 (no) and 1 (yes)
Child receiving psychological counseling:
  0 (no) and 1 (yes)
Child's current living situation:
  0 (out of home) and 1 (parent's home)
Siblings of child are known victims of sexual abuse:
  0 (no) and 1 (yes)
Child involved in concurrent dependency and neglect case:
  0 (no) and 1 (yes)
Child testified in concurrent dependency and neglect case:
  0 (no) and 1 (yes)
Defendant's age (in years)
Defendant's gender:
  1 (male) and 2 (female)
Defendant's race/ethnicity:
  1 (majority) and 2 (minority)
Defendant's initial stance on the abuse:
  1 (denial), 2 (admission but takes no responsibility, e.g., drunk and
    blanked out), 3 (accepts full responsibility)
Defendant's final stance on the abuse:
  1 (denial), 2 (admission but takes no responsibility, e.g., drunk and
    blanked out), 3 (accepts full responsibility)
Number of perpetrators
Type of relationship scale:

1 (stranger), 2 (known but not in position of trust), 3 (position of trust), 4 (parent or stepparent)

Type of sexual abuse scale:
1 (exhibitionism), 2 (nongenital), 3 (genital but no penetration), 4 (penetration)

Injury scale:
1 (none), 2 (mild), 3 (moderate), 4 (severe)

Force scale:
1 (none), 2 (mild), 3 (moderate), 4 (severe)

Duration of abuse scale:
1 (1 day), 2 (2 days–6 months), 3 (6 months–5 years), 4 (over 5 years)

Severity of abuse scale:
Sum of scores for type of sexual activity, injury, force, and duration of abuse scales

Outcome of case:
0 (not guilty) and 1 (guilty, plea bargain)

Outcome of trial:
1 (not guilty, hung jury) and 2 (guilty)

Sentence:
1 (deferred judgment or sentence), 2 (probation, no incarceration), 3 (county jail), 4 (prison)

Defendant found guilty of other charges:
0 (no) and 1 (yes)

Child experienced other significant traumas since sexual assault:
0 (no) and 1 (yes)

Child/family threatened since assault:
1 (no threat), 2 (moderate, e.g., harassment, ostracism), 3 (extreme, e.g., kidnapping, murder)

Likelihood that sexual abuse took place:
1 (extremely likely), 2 (likely), 3 (uncertain), 4 (unlikely), 5 (extremely unlikely)

Likelihood that defendant is the person who sexually abused the child:
1 (extremely likely), 2 (likely), 3 (uncertain), 4 (unlikely), 5 (extremely unlikely)

Socioeconomic Status (SES) (Watt, 1976; adaptation of Hollingshead Scale)
Seven-point scale:
1 (high SES) and 7 (low SES)

Child Behavior Checklist (Achenbach & Edelbrock, 1983)
Total *T* score
Internalizing *T* score
Externalizing *T* score
Improvement:
0 (no) and 1 (yes)

Teacher Report Form (Achenbach & Edelbrock, 1986)
   Total *T* score

Social Adjustment Scale–Revised (Weissman et al., 1978)
   Mean total score

Spielberger State Anxiety Score (Spielberger et al., 1970; Spielberger, 1973)
   Mean total score

Before-Court Measure
   Court appearance number
   Total number of family/friends waiting with the child
   Where child waited
   Amount of time child waited before entering courtroom
   Feelings about going to court:
      Verbal response, positive (1), ambivalent/neutral (2), negative (3)
      Faces scale, 1 (very happy), 2 (happy), 3 (unhappy), 4 (very unhappy)
   Feelings about possibility of primary caretaker in courtroom:
      Verbal response, positive (1), ambivalent/neutral (2), negative (3)
      Faces scale, 1 (very happy), 2 (happy), 3 (unhappy), 4 (very unhappy)
   Feelings about talking to judge:
      Verbal response, positive (1), ambivalent/neutral (2), negative (3)
      Faces scale, 1 (very happy), 2 (happy), 3 (unhappy), 4 (very unhappy)
   Feelings about talking to prosecutor:
      Verbal response, positive (1), ambivalent/neutral (2), negative (3)
      Faces scale, 1 (very happy), 2 (happy), 3 (unhappy), 4 (very unhappy)
   Feelings about talking to defense attorney:
      Verbal response, positive (1), ambivalent/neutral (2), negative (3)
      Faces scale, 1 (very happy), 2 (happy), 3 (unhappy), 4 (very unhappy)
   Feelings about seeing defendant in court:
      Verbal response, positive (1), ambivalent/neutral (2), negative (3)
      Faces scale, 1 (very happy), 2 (happy), 3 (unhappy), 4 (very unhappy)
   Feelings about telling the jury what happened:
      Verbal response, positive (1), ambivalent/neutral (2), negative (3)
      Faces scale, 1 (very happy), 2 (happy), 3 (unhappy), 4 (very unhappy)

Day of Court Measure
   Total score

Courtroom Observation Measure
   Type of court appearance
   Number of times child has already testified
   Child's mood:
      1 (very happy), 2 (happy), 3 (neutral), 4 (sad), 5 (very sad)
   Child's self-confidence:
      1 (very unconfident), 2 (unconfident), 3 (neutral), 4 (confident), 5 (very confident)

Child's confidence of statements:
   1 (very unconfident), 2 (unconfident), 3 (neutral), 4 (confident), 5 (very confident)
Child's anxiety:
   1 (very relaxed), 2 (relaxed), 3 (neutral), 4 (anxious/fearful), 5 (very anxious/fearful)
Child's sympathy/anger toward defendant:
   1 (very sympathetic), 2 (somewhat sympathetic), 3 (neutral), 4 (somewhat angry), 5 (very angry)
Child's cooperativeness/anger with attorney:
   1 (very cooperative), 2 (cooperative), 3 (neutral), 4 (angry), 5 (very angry)
Child's speech fluency:
   1 (very faltering), 2 (somewhat faltering), 3 (relatively fluent), 4 (very fluent)
Child's audibility/inaudibility:
   1 (loud), 2 (audible), 3 (barely audible), 4 (inaudible)
Child's ability to answer questions:
   1 (silent or only said "I don't know"), 2 (answered some questions),
   3 (answered most questions), 4 (answered all questions)
Child's resistance/susceptibility to leading questions:
   1 (very resistant), 2 (resistant), 3 (influenced), 4 (very influenced)
Child's spontaneous detail provided to attorney's questions:
   1 (no detail), 2 (little detail), 3 (some detail), 4 (a lot of detail)
Recantation of assault:
   0 (no) and 1 (yes)
Recantation of identity of perpetrator:
   0 (no) and 1 (yes)
Child provided inconsistent testimony about main actions of assault:
   0 (no) and 1 (yes)
Child provided inconsistent testimony about frequency of assault:
   0 (no) and 1 (yes)
Child provided inconsistent testimony about where assault occurred:
   0 (no) and 1 (yes)
Child provided inconsistent testimony about when assault occurred:
   0 (no) and 1 (yes)
Child provided inconsistent testimony about peripheral details:
   0 (no) and 1 (yes)
Attorney's use of leading questions:
   1 (no leading questions), 2 (some leading questions), 3 (many leading questions), 4 (almost exclusively leading questions)
Attorney's focus:
   1 (mainly assault or central information), 2 (peripheral details),
   3 (irrelevancies)
Age-appropriate language of attorney's questions:
   1 (virtually all questions age inappropriate), 2 (most questions age inappropriate), 3 (half age appropriate, half not), 4 (most questions age appropriate), 5 (virtually all questions age appropriate)

Age-appropriate content of attorney's questions:
> 1 (virtually all questions age inappropriate), 2 (most questions age inappropriate), 3 (half age appropriate, half not), 4 (most questions age appropriate), 5 (virtually all questions age appropriate)

Child cried:
> 1 (no), 2 (a little), 3 (a lot)

Child's credibility:
> 1 (not at all credible), 2 (not very credible), 3 (credible), 4 (highly credible)

Child's overall demeanor:
> 1 (very calm), 2 (calm), 3 (some distress), 4 (very distressed)

Child's fear of defendant:
> 1 (very unfrightened), 2 (unfrightened), 3 (neutral), 4 (frightened), 5 (very frightened)

Child permitted to sit on parent's/supportive other's lap:
> 0 (no) and 1 (yes)

Child permitted to hold a toy:
> 0 (no) and 1 (yes)

Child permitted to testify with aid of props:
> 0 (no) and 1 (yes)

Child permitted to testify via videotape:
> 0 (no) and 1 (yes)

Defendant seated out of view:
> 0 (no) and 1 (yes)

Child's testimony given in judge's chambers:
> 0 (no) and 1 (yes)

Child's testimony given via closed-circuit television:
> 0 (no) and 1 (yes)

Courtroom cleared of spectators:
> 0 (no) and 1 (yes)

Parent/loved one permitted to remain in courtroom:
> 0 (no) and 1 (yes)

Victim assistant permitted to remain in courtroom:
> 0 (no) and 1 (yes)

Judge questioned child about competency:
> 0 (no) and 1 (yes)

Child deemed competent:
> 0 (no) and 1 (yes)

Judge actively took steps to protect the child:
> 0 (no) and 1 (yes)

Judge actively took steps that would increase child's discomfort:
> 0 (no) and 1 (yes)

Judge was passive in his/her dealings with the child:
> 0 (no) and 1 (yes)

Judge questioned child about factual information:
> 0 (no) and 1 (yes)

Judge asks for clarifying information from child:
  0 (no) and 1 (yes)
Attorney's demeanor toward child:
  1 (very supportive), 2 (supportive), 3 (neutral), 4 (unsupportive), 5 (very unsupportive)
Judge's demeanor toward child:
  1 (very supportive), 2 (supportive), 3 (neutral), 4 (unsupportive), 5 (very unsupportive)
Trial to jury:
  0 (no) and 1 (yes)
Other events adding to child's possible stress:
  0 (no) and 1 (yes)
Defendant present in courtroom when child testified:
  0 (no) and 1 (yes)
Approximate number of people in courtroom when child testified:
  1 (1–10), 2 (11–20), 3 (21–30), 4 (31–40), 5 (41–50)
Total length of time child was in court
Length of time child was placed under direct examination
Length of time child was placed under cross-examination
Length of time child was placed under redirect examination
Length of time child was placed under re-cross-examination
Length of time judge questioned child
Number of recesses
Length of recesses

After-Court Measure
Feelings about having gone to court:
  Verbal response, positive (1), ambivalent/neutral (2), negative (3)
  Faces scale, 1 (very happy), 2 (happy), 3 (unhappy), 4 (very unhappy)
Feelings about primary caretaker having been/not been in courtroom:
  Verbal response, positive (1), ambivalent/neutral (2), negative (3)
  Faces scale, 1 (very happy), 2 (happy), 3 (unhappy), 4 (very unhappy)
Feelings about having talked to judge:
  Verbal response, positive (1), ambivalent/neutral (2), negative (3)
  Faces scale, 1 (very happy), 2 (happy), 3 (unhappy), 4 (very unhappy)
Feelings about having talked to prosecutor:
  Verbal response, positive (1), ambivalent/neutral (2), negative (3)
  Faces scale, 1 (very happy), 2 (happy), 3 (unhappy), 4 (very unhappy)
Feelings about having talked to defense attorney:
  Verbal response, positive (1), ambivalent/neutral (2), negative (3)
  Faces scale, 1 (very happy), 2 (happy), 3 (unhappy), 4 (very unhappy)
Feelings about having seen defendant in court:
  Verbal response, positive (1), ambivalent/neutral (2), negative (3)
  Faces scale, 1 (very happy), 2 (happy), 3 (unhappy), 4 (very unhappy)
Feelings about having told the jury what happened:

Verbal response, positive (1), ambivalent/neutral (2), negative (3)

Faces scale, 1 (very happy), 2 (happy), 3 (unhappy), 4 (very unhappy)

What could have made the child more comfortable? (write in)

Legal Involvement Questionnaire[10]

Did the child testify?

0 (no) and 1 (yes)

Overall effect of testifying/not testifying:

1 (very positive), 2 (somewhat positive), 3 (somewhat negative), 4 (very negative)

Satisfaction with case outcome (caretaker asked to indicate separately satisfaction for self and for child):

1 (very unsatisfied), 2 (somewhat unsatisfied), 3 (somewhat satisfied), 4 (very satisfied)

Interactions with legal personnel (separate judgment made for victim advocate, prosecuting attorney, defense attorney, judge, social worker, police, guardian ad litem, district attorney investigator, researchers, and "other"):

1 (very positive), 2 (somewhat positive), 3 (somewhat negative), 4 (very negative)

Has child ever testified in any other legal proceeding aside from this case (caretaker answers only):

0 (no) and 1 (yes)

Effect of legal process (caretaker answers only):

Marital relationship improved:

0 (no) and 1 (yes)

Marital problems:

0 (no) and 1 (yes)

Worked extra hours:

0 (no) and 1 (yes)

Missed time at work:

0 (no) and 1 (yes)

Increased income:

0 (no) and 1 (yes)

Loss of income:

0 (no) and 1 (yes)

Brought family closer together:

0 (no) and 1 (yes)

Family arguments:

0 (no) and 1 (yes)

Child behavior improved:

0 (no) and 1 (yes)

Child behavior worse:

0 (no) and 1 (yes)

[10] For questions children answered on the Legal Involvement Questionnaire, the terms "positive" and "negative" were replaced with "good" and "bad," respectively.

Strengthened faith in God:
  0 (no) and 1 (yes)
Lessened faith in God:
  0 (no) and 1 (yes)
Friendships strengthened:
  0 (no) and 1 (yes)
Friendships strained:
  0 (no) and 1 (yes)
Increased social contacts outside family:
  0 (no) and 1 (yes)
Decreased social contacts outside family:
  0 (no) and 1 (yes)
Overall effect of participation in criminal investigation and prosecution on
    caretaker's/child's life (caretaker completed separately for self and
    child):
  1 (very positive), 2 (somewhat positive), 3 (somewhat negative), 4 (very
    negative)
Fairness/unfairness of criminal justice system:
  1 (very fair), 2 (somewhat fair), 3 (somewhat unfair), 4 (very unfair)
Speed/slowness of the criminal justice system:
  1 (very fast), 2 (somewhat fast), 3 (somewhat slow), 4 (very slow)
Communication about the case (caretaker answers only):
  1 (very informed), 2 (somewhat informed), 3 (somewhat uninformed),
    4 (very uninformed)
How many times has child been questioned about the assault by officials,
    not counting days in court (e.g., by police, detectives, social workers,
    lawyers) (caretaker answers only)
What changes needed in legal process? (write in)

Case Progress
Number of continuances
Number of continuances involving the child
Number of times child came to the courthouse (subpoenaed)
Number of times child testified
Length of the legal process
Length of time from disclosure to preliminary hearing
Length of time from preliminary hearing to trial or plea bargain
Length of time from trial or plea bargain to sentencing
Did the case "close" (reach conclusion) before the end of the study:
  0 (no) and 1 (yes)
Defendant still at large:
  0 (no) and 1 (yes)

REFERENCES

Achenbach, T. M., & Edelbrock, C. (1983). *Manual for the Child Behavior Checklist and the Revised Child Behavior Profile.* Burlington: University of Vermont.

Achenbach, T. M., & Edelbrock, C. (1986). *Manual for the Teacher's Report Form and teacher version of the Child Behavior Profile.* Burlington: University of Vermont.

Achenbach, T. M., McConaughy, S. H., & Howell, C. T. (1987). Child/adolescent behavioral and emotional problems: Implications of cross-informant correlations for situational specificity. *Psychological Bulletin, 101,* 213–232.

Alleged rape victim sues over parole. (1991, July 7). *Los Angeles Times,* sec. A, p. 26.

American Association for Protecting Children. (1988). *Highlights of official child neglect and abuse reporting, 1986.* Denver: American Humane Association.

Andrews, F. M., & Withey, S. B. (1976). *Social indicators of well-being.* New York: Plenum.

Attorney General's Task Force on Family Violence. (1984). Washington, DC: Department of Justice.

Benedek, E. P. (1982). The role of the child psychiatrist in court cases involving child victims of sexual assault. *Journal of the American Academy of Child Psychiatry, 21,* 519–520.

Berliner, L., & Barbieri, M. K. (1984). The testimony of the child victim of sexual assault. *Journal of Social Issues, 40,* 125–137.

Bottoms, B. L., & Goodman, G. S. (1989, April). *The credibility of child victims of sexual assault.* Paper presented at the meeting of the Eastern Psychological Association, Boston.

Bowlby, J. (1980). *Attachment and loss: Vol. 3. Loss, sadness, and depression.* New York: Basic.

Browne, A., & Finkelhor, D. (1986). Impact of child sexual abuse: A review of the research. *Psychological Bulletin, 99,* 66–77.

Brownmiller, S. (1975). *Against our will: Men, women, and rape.* New York: Bantam.

Bulkley, J. (1982). *Recommendations for improving legal intervention in intra-family child sexual abuse cases.* Washington, DC: American Bar Association.

Bulkley, J. (1983). *Child sexual abuse and the law.* Washington, DC: American Bar Association.

Burgess, A. W., & Holmstrom, L. L. (1978). The child and the family during the court process. In A. Burgess, A. N. Groth, L. L. Holmstrom, & S. M. Sgori (Eds.), *Sexual assault of children and adolescents.* Lexington, MA: Heath.

Bussey, K., Lee, K., & Ross, C. (1991, April). Factors influencing children's lying and truthfulness. In M. DeSimone & M. Toglia (Chairs), *Lying and truthfulness among young children: Implications for their truthfulness in legal proceedings.* Symposium conducted at the meeting of the Society for Research in Child Development, Seattle.

Cashmore, J., & Bussey, K. (1990). Children's construction of court proceedings. In J.

Spencer, G. Nicholson, R. Flin, & R. Bull (Eds.), *Children's evidence in legal proceedings.* Cambridge: Cambridge University Press.

Claman, L., Harris, J. C., Bernstein, B. E., & Lovitt, R. (1986). The adolescent as a witness in a case of incest: Assessment and outcome. *Journal of the American Academy of Child Psychiatry,* **25,** 457–461.

Clarke-Stewart, A., Thompson, W., & Lepore, S. (1989, April). Manipulating children's interpretations through interrogation. In G. S. Goodman (Chair), *Do children provide accurate eyewitness reports? Research and social policy implications.* Symposium conducted at the meeting of the Society for Research in Child Development, Kansas City, MO.

Cohen, R. L., & Harnick, M. A. (1980). The susceptibility of child witnesses to suggestion: An empirical study. *Law and Human Behavior,* **4,** 201–210.

Conte, J., & Berliner, L. (1984). *The sexual assault profile.* Unpublished manuscript, University of Washington, School of Social Work, Seattle.

Conte, J., & Berliner, L. (1988). The impact of sexual abuse on children. In L. Walker (Ed.), *Handbook of child sexual abuse.* New York: Springer.

Conte, J., & Schuerman, J. R. (1987). Factors associated with an increased impact of child sexual abuse. *Child Abuse and Neglect,* **11,** 201–212.

Coy v. Iowa, 56 U.S.L.W. 1931 (1988).

Craig v. Maryland, 332 Md. 418, 588 A.2d 281 (1991).

David, H. (1990). The role of youth interrogator. In J. Spencer, G. Nicholson, R. Flin, & R. Bull (Eds.), *Children's evidence in legal proceedings.* Cambridge: Cambridge University Press.

DeFrancis, V. (1969). *Protecting the child victim of sex crimes committed by adults.* Denver: American Humane Association.

Dent, H. (1977). Stress as a factor influencing person recognition in identification parades. *Bulletin of the British Psychological Society,* **30,** 339–340.

Dent, H., & Flin, R. (1992). *Children as witnesses.* London: Wiley.

Department of Health and Human Services. (1992). *National child abuse and neglect data system working paper: 1990 summary components* (HHS [ACF] 92-30361). Washington, DC.

Douglas, J. W. B. (1975). Early hospital admissions and later disturbances of behavior and learning. *Developmental Medicine and Child Neurology,* **17,** 456–480.

Duggan, L. M., Aubrey, M., Doherty, E., Isquith, P., Levine, M., & Scheiner, J. (1989). The credibility of children as witnesses in a simulated child sex abuse trial. In S. Ceci, M. Toglia, & D. Ross (Eds.), *Perspectives on children's testimony.* New York: Springer.

Dunn, J. (1988). Normative life events as risk factors in childhood. In M. Rutter (Ed.), *Studies of psychosocial risk: The power of longitudinal data.* New York: Cambridge University Press.

Edelbrock, C. S., & Achenbach, T. (1984). The teacher version of the Child Behavior Profile: 1. Boys aged 6–11. *Journal of Consulting and Clinical Psychology,* **52,** 207–217.

Elder, G. H. (1979). Historical change in life patterns and personality. In P. Baltes & O. G. Brim (Eds.), *Life span development and behavior* (Vol. **2**). New York: Academic.

Everson, M. D., Hunter, W. M., Runyan, D. K., Edelsohn, G. A., & Coulter, M. L. (1989). Maternal support following disclosure of incest. *American Journal of Orthopsychiatry,* **59,** 197–207.

Ferguson, B. F. (1979). Preparing young children for hospitalization: A comparison of two methods. *Pediatrics,* **64,** 656–664.

Finkelhor, D. (1984). *Child sexual abuse.* New York: Free Press.

Friedman, W. J. (1982). *The developmental psychology of time.* New York: Academic.

Friedrich, W. N., Grambsch, P., Damon, L., Hewitt, S. K., Koverola, C., Lang, R., &

Wolfe, V. (1991). *The child sexual behavior inventory: Normative and clinical comparisons.* Unpublished manuscript, Mayo Clinic, Rochester, MN.

Garmezy, N. (1983). Stressors of childhood. In N. Garmezy & M. Rutter (Eds.), *Stress, coping, and development in children.* New York: McGraw-Hill.

Garmezy, N., & Rutter, M. (Eds.). (1983). *Stress, coping, and development in children.* New York: McGraw-Hill.

Gibbens, T. C. N., & Prince, J. (1963). *Child victims of sex crimes.* London: Institute for the Study and Treatment of Delinquency.

Gilligan, C. (1982). *In a different voice.* Cambridge, MA: Harvard University Press.

Goldman, R., & Goldman, J. (1982). *Children's sexual thinking.* London: Routledge & Kegan Paul.

Goodman, G. S. (Ed.). (1984). The child witness. *Journal of Social Issues,* **40**(2).

Goodman, G. S., & Aman, C. (1990). Children's use of anatomically detailed dolls to recall an event. *Child Development,* **61,** 1859–1871.

Goodman, G. S., Aman, C., & Hirschman, J. (1987). Child sexual and physical abuse: Children's testimony. In S. Ceci, M. Toglia, & D. Ross (Eds.), *Children's eyewitness memory.* New York: Springer.

Goodman, G. S., & Bottoms, B. L. (in press). *Child victims, child witnesses: Understanding and improving children's eyewitness testimony.* New York: Guilford.

Goodman, G. S., Bottoms, B. L., Herscovici, B., & Shaver, P. (1989). Determinants of the child victim's perceived credibility. In S. Ceci, M. Toglia, & D. Ross (Eds.), *Perspectives on children's testimony.* New York: Springer.

Goodman, G. S., Levine, M., Melton, G. B., & Ogden, D. W. (1990). Child witnesses and the confrontation clause: The American Psychological Association brief in Maryland v. Craig. *Law and Human Behavior,* **15,** 13–29.

Goodman, G. S., & Reed, R. (1986). Age differences in eyewitness testimony. *Law and Human Behavior,* **10,** 317–332.

Goodman, G. S., & Rosenberg, M. (1987). The child witness to family violence. In D. Sonkin (Ed.), *Domestic violence on trial.* New York: Springer.

Goodman, G. S., Rudy, L., Bottoms, B. L., & Aman, C. (1990). Children's memory and concerns: Ecological issues in the study of children's testimony. In R. Fivush & J. Hudson (Eds.), *Knowing and remembering in young children.* New York: Cambridge University Press.

Gore, S. (1985). Social support and styles of coping with stress. In S. Cohen & S. L. Syme (Eds.), *Social support and health.* New York: Academic.

Gray, E. (1988). The child victim in criminal court. *Looking Ahead,* **2,** 1–4.

Harnon, E. (1990). Children's evidence in the Israeli criminal justice system with special emphasis on sexual offenses. In J. Spencer, G. Nicholson, R. Flin, & R. Bull (Eds.), *Children's evidence in legal proceedings.* Cambridge: Cambridge University Press.

Harris, J. C., King, S. L., Reifler, J. P., & Rosenberg, L. A. (1984). Emotional and learning disorders in 6- to 12-year-old boys attending special schools. *Journal of the American Academy of Child Psychiatry,* **23,** 431–437.

Hetherington, E. M., Clingempeel, W. G., Anderson, E. R., Deal, J. E., Stanley Hagan, M., Hollier, E. A., & Lindner, M. S. (1992). Coping with marital transitions: A family systems perspective. *Monographs of the Society for Research in Child Development,* **57**(2–3, Serial No. 227).

Hill, P. E., & Hill, S. M. (1987). Videotaping children's testimony: An empirical view. *Michigan Law Review,* **85,** 809–833.

Hollingshead, A. B., & Redlich, F. C. (1958). *Social class and mental illness.* New York: Wiley.

Kail, R. (1989). *Memory development.* New York: Freeman.

Katz, S., & Mazur, M. A. (1979). *Understanding the rape victim.* New York: Wiley.

Leippe, M. R., Brigham, J. C., Cousins, C., & Romanczyk, A. (1989). The opinions and practices of criminal attorneys regarding child eyewitnesses: A survey. In S. Ceci, D. F. Ross, & M. P. Toglia (Eds.), *Perspectives on children's testimony.* New York: Springer.

Leippe, M. R., & Romanczyk, A. (1987). Children on the witness stand: A communication/persuasion analysis of jurors' reactions to child witnesses. In S. Ceci, M. P. Toglia, & D. F. Ross (Eds.), *Children's eyewitness memory.* New York: Springer.

Leippe, M., Romanczyk, A., & Manion, A. (1991). Eyewitness memory for a touching experience: Accuracy differences between child and adult witnesses. *Journal of Applied Psychology,* **76,** 367–379.

Levine, M., & Levine, A. (1992). *Helping children: A social history.* New York: Oxford University Press.

Libai, D. (1969). The protection of the child victim of a sexual offense in the criminal justice system. *Wayne State Law Review,* **15,** 977–1032.

Limber, S., & Etheredge, S. (1989, August). Prosecutors' perceptions of sexually abused children as witnesses. In G. S. Goodman (Chair), *Child abuse victims in court.* Symposium conducted at the meeting of the American Psychological Association, New Orleans.

Lipovsky, J., Tidwell, R. P., Kilpatrick, D. G., Saunders, F. F., & Dawson, V. L. (1991, August). *Children as witnesses in criminal court: Examination of current practices.* Paper presented at the meeting of the American Psychological Association, San Francisco.

Maccoby, E. (1983). Social-emotional development and response to stressors. In N. Garmezy & M. Rutter (Eds.), *Stress, coping, and development in children.* New York: McGraw-Hill.

Marin, B. V., Holmes, D. L., Guth, M., & Kovac, P. (1979). The potential of children as eyewitnesses. *Law and Human Behavior,* **3,** 295–305.

Maryland v. Craig, 110 S. Ct. 3157 (1990).

Melton, G. B. (1989, August). Children's knowledge, reasoning, and attitudes about the legal process. In G. S. Goodman (Chair), *Child abuse victims in court.* Symposium conducted at the meeting of the American Psychological Association, New Orleans.

Melton, G. B., & Berliner, L. (1992). *Preparing sexually abused children for testimony: Children's perceptions of the legal process* (Final report to the National Center on Child Abuse and Neglect, Washington, DC).

Moston, S. (1987, September). *The effects of the provisions of social support in child interviews.* Paper presented at the meeting of the British Psychological Association, York, England.

Musick, J. S., Stott, F. M., Spencer, K. K., Goldman, J., & Cohler, B. J. (1987). Maternal factors related to vulnerability and resiliency in young children at risk. In E. J. Anthony & B. J. Cohler (Eds.), *The invulnerable child.* New York: Guilford.

Nelson, K. (1986). *Event memory: Function and structure in development.* Hillsdale, NJ: Erlbaum.

Oates, R., & Tong, L. (1987). Sexual abuse of children: An area with room for professional reforms. *Medical Journal of Australia,* **147,** 544–548.

Parker, J. (1982). The rights of child witnesses: Is the court a protector or perpetrator? *New England Law Review,* **17,** 643–717.

Peters, D. (1988, March). The effects of event-stress and stress during lineup identification on eyewitness accuracy in children. In D. Peters (Chair), *Children's eyewitness testimony.* Symposium conducted at the meeting of the American Psychology and Law Society, Miami.

Pierre-Puysegur, M. A. (1985, July). *Representations of the penal system among 6- to 10-year-old children*. Paper presented at the eighth biennial meeting of the International Society for the Study of Behavioral Development, Tours, France.

Pipe, M. E., & Goodman, G. S. (1991). Elements of secrecy: Implications for children's testimony. *Behavioral Sciences and the Law, 9,* 33–41.

Pynoos, R., & Eth, S. (1984). The child witness to homicide. *Journal of Social Issues, 40,* 87–108.

Quinton, D., & Rutter, M. (1976). Early hospital admissions and later disturbances of behaviour. An attempted replication of Douglas' findings. *Developmental Medicine and Child Neurology, 18,* 447–459.

Rogers, C. M. (1980, September). *Child sexual abuse and the courts: Empirical findings.* Paper presented at the meeting of the American Psychological Association, Montreal.

Rohner, R. P., & Rohner, E. C. (1980). Antecedents and consequences of parental rejection: A theory of emotional abuse. *Child Abuse and Neglect, 4,* 189–198.

Ross, D. M., & Ross, S. A. (1988). *Childhood pain.* Baltimore: Urban & Schwarzenberg.

Runyan, D. K., Everson, M. D., Edelsohn, G. A., Hunter, W. M., & Coulter, M. L. (1988). Impact of legal intervention on sexually abused children. *Journal of Pediatrics, 113,* 647–653.

Rush, F. (1980). *The best kept secret: Sexual abuse of children.* New York: McGraw-Hill.

Russell, D. (1983). The incidence and prevalence of intrafamilial and extrafamilial sexual abuse of female children. *Child Abuse and Neglect, 7,* 133–146.

Rutter, M. (1971). Parent-child separation: Psychological effects on the children. *Journal of Child Psychology and Psychiatry, 12,* 233–260.

Rutter, M. (1983). Stress, coping, and development: Some issues and some questions. In N. Garmezy & M. Rutter (Eds.), *Stress, coping, and development in children.* New York: McGraw-Hill.

Sas, L. (1991). *Reducing the system-induced trauma for child sexual abuse victims through court preparation, assessment, and follow-up.* London, ON: London Family Court.

Sas, L., & Wolfe, D. (1991, August). Preparing sexually abused children for the stress of court. In G. S. Goodman (Chair), *Assessment, diagnosis, and support of child sexual abuse victims.* Symposium conducted at the meeting of the American Psychological Association, San Francisco.

Saywitz, K. (1989). Children's conceptions of the legal system: "Court is a place to play basketball." In S. Ceci, M. Toglia, & D. Ross (Eds.), *Perspectives on children's testimony.* New York: Springer.

Saywitz, K., Goodman, G. S., Nichols, E., & Moan, S. (1991). Children's memories of physical examinations involving genital touch: Implications for reports of child sexual abuse. *Journal of Consulting and Clinical Psychology, 59,* 682–691.

Schudson, C. B. (1987). Making courts safe for children. *Journal of Interpersonal Violence, 2,* 120–122.

Smith, B. (1991, March). *The prosecution of child maltreatment cases.* Paper presented at the grantee meeting of the National Center on Child Abuse and Neglect, Washington, DC.

Spencer, J., & Flin, R. (1990). *The evidence of children.* London: Blackstone.

Spielberger, C. D. (1973). *Preliminary test manual for the State-Trait Anxiety Inventory for Children.* Palo Alto, CA: Consulting Psychologists Press.

Spielberger, C. D., Gorsuch, R. L., & Lushene, R. E. (1970). *Manual for the State-Trait Anxiety Inventory.* Palo Alto, CA: Consulting Psychologists Press.

Swim, J. K., Borgida, E., & McCoy, K. (1991, August). *Children's videotaped testimony and jury decision making.* Paper presented at the meeting of the American Psychological Association, San Francisco.

Tedesco, J. F., & Schnell, S. V. (1987). Children's reactions to sex abuse investigation and litigation. *Child Abuse and Neglect, 11,* 267–272.

Terr, L. C. (1990). *Too scared to cry.* New York: Harper & Row.

Terr, L. C., & Watson, A. S. (1980). The battered child rebrutalized: Ten cases of medical-legal confusion. In G. J. Williams & J. Money (Eds.), *Traumatic abuse and neglect of children at home.* Baltimore: Johns Hopkins University Press.

Tidwell, R., & Lipovsky, J. (1991). *Child victims and child witnesses: A three-state profile* (Final Report to the State Justice Institute [Grant 88-11J-D-064], Alexandria, VA).

Warren-Leubecker, A., Tate, C., Hinton, I., & Ozbek, N. (1989). What do children know about the legal system and when do they know it? First steps down a less traveled path in child witness research. In S. Ceci, M. Toglia, & D. Ross (Eds.), *Perspectives on children's testimony.* New York: Springer.

Watt, N. (1976). *Two-factor index of social position: Amherst modification.* Unpublished manuscript, Department of Psychology, University of Denver.

Weiss, E. H., & Berg, R. F. (1982). Child victims of sexual assault: Impact of court procedures. *Journal of the American Academy of Child Psychiatry, 21,* 513–518.

Weissman, M. M., & Bothwell, S. (1976). Assessment of social adjustment by patient self-report. *Archives of General Psychiatry, 33,* 1111–1115.

Weissman, M. M., Prusoff, B. A., Thompson, W. D., Harding, P. S., & Myers, J. K. (1978). Social adjustment by self-report in a community sample of psychiatric outpatients. *Journal of Nervous and Mental Disease, 166,* 317–326.

Wells, G., & Leippe, M. R. (1981). How do triers of fact infer the accuracy of eyewitness identification? Using memory for peripheral detail can be misleading. *Journal of Applied Psychology, 66,* 682–687.

Whitcomb, D., & Runyan, D. (1992, January). *Effects of the court system on child victims as witnesses.* Paper presented at the Conference on Responding to Child Maltreatment, San Diego.

Whitcomb, D., Shapiro, E., & Stellwagen, L. (1985). *When the victim is a child: Issues for judges and prosecutors.* Washington, DC: U.S. Department of Justice.

Wolfe, D. A., & Mosk, M. D. (1983). Behavioral comparisons of children from abusive and distressed families. *Journal of Consulting and Clinical Psychology, 51,* 702–708.

Wyatt, G. E., & Powell, G. J. (Eds.). (1988). *Lasting effects of child sexual abuse.* Newbury Park, CA: Sage.

ACKNOWLEDGMENTS

We are grateful to many people for their help. The study would not have been possible without the support of the Denver, Arapahoe, and Adams County District Attorneys' Offices. In Denver, we are especially grateful to Karen Steinhauser, chief deputy district attorney of the Domestic Violence Unit, and her entire staff; Steve Siegel, director of program development; and Norman S. Early, Jr., Denver County district attorney. In Arapahoe, we enjoyed the support of John Jordan, chief deputy district attorney, and Jim Peters, deputy district attorney, both of whom provided invaluable assistance; the entire staff of the Victim Advocates Office, especially Sher Halford; and Robert Gallagher, Jr., Arapahoe County district attorney. In Adams, we thank Robert Grant, chief deputy district attorney; the entire staff of the Victim Advocates Office, in particular Natalie Maier and Betty North; and James F. Smith, Adams County district attorney. Kitty Arnold, director of the Arapahoe County Department of Social Services, also facilitated our study. Ralph Mason, Shelley Bresnick, Shelle Kraft, Annette Hahn, and Michelle Allen provided valuable research assistance, and Drs. Phillip Shaver, Harry Gollob, Marshall Haith, and Kenneth Levy offered helpful editorial advice and statistical consultations. Two anonymous reviewers offered a number of insightful suggestions concerning an earlier draft of this *Monograph*. We also express gratitude to the National Institute of Justice, especially Dr. Richard Titus and Dr. George Schollenberger, for overseeing the project. Finally, special thanks go to the children and families who participated in our research.

Measures reported in this paper are available on request from the first author.

This project was supported by a grant from the National Institute of Justice (85-IJ-CX-0020) to Dr. Gail S. Goodman. Correspondence concerning this research should be addressed to Dr. Gail Goodman, Department of Psychology, University of California, Davis, CA 95616.

STEPS TOWARD FORENSICALLY RELEVANT RESEARCH

John E. B. Myers

The research described in this *Monograph* is an important step forward in our understanding of children as witnesses. The research provides valuable empirical support for reforms designed to make testifying less stressful for children. Although reducing children's stress is a worthy goal, the lasting importance of this research lies not in the finding that testifying is stressful or in the support that the research provides for techniques to reduce children's stress. In the final analysis, the most important contribution of this research is the discovery that, for some children, testifying in the traditional manner interferes with the child's ability to answer questions, thus undermining the very purpose of the trial—discovery of truth. This finding, more than any other, will improve the ability of the legal system to foster children's emotional well-being while protecting the rights of individuals accused of child abuse.

A Lawyer's-Eye View of Litigation

Psychologists, physicians, and social workers sometimes wonder at the machinations of lawyers. The gulf that so often separates lawyers from other professionals is not surprising when one contrasts the training and experience of the lawyer with that of the researcher, mental health professional, or physician. To place the research in this *Monograph* in context, it is useful to dwell momentarily on the perspective that lawyers bring to the courtroom.

In medieval England, certain legal disputes could be resolved through trial by battle. Litigants retained professional men-at-arms to wage battle under the watchful eye of the king's judges (Blackstone, 1765). Vestiges of trial by battle linger in today's legal system. The professional soldier has become a lawyer. The suit of mail is now a three-piece suit. Sharp steel has given way to sharp words. Like the contest of old, however, modern trials are highly adversarial.

Although the comparison of modern trials to trial by battle is exaggerated, the similarities provide a measure of insight into today's criminal justice system. Modern criminal trials are firmly grounded on the adversary model, where the goal is victory. In presenting evidence, attorneys do not strive for balance, nor do they attempt to paint the entire picture of what occurred. Rather, each attorney presents the evidence most favorable to his or her client. Cross-examination is conceived by many attorneys in martial terms, as a weapon deployed to undermine the opponent's case. The judge administers a complex set of rules designed to ensure a "fair fight." When all the evidence has been presented—when the dust of battle has settled— the jury considers the competing claims and renders a verdict. The theory of the adversary system is that the truth emerges from the orchestrated clash of opposing views.

Additional insight into the perspective of many prosecutors and criminal defense attorneys comes with an understanding of the lawyer's single-minded loyalty to the client. Clients are entitled to zealous representation (American Bar Association, 1969, 1983). No group of attorneys takes the responsibility of zealous representation more seriously than defense attorneys. For defense counsel, the presumption of innocence is more than a platitude; it is a creed. Wolfram writes: "A defense lawyer's main responsibility is to further the interests of his or her client as defined by the client. Typically the client's interest is to obtain the least costly sanction and an acquittal of all charges if possible. . . . The lawyer's knowledge that the client is guilty does not substantially affect the kind of defense that should be afforded" (1986, p. 590).

In view of the professional responsibility to put the client's interests first, it is not surprising that defense attorneys take aim at witnesses called by the prosecution, including children. Defense attorneys do not relish attacking children's credibility. Nevertheless, the defense attorney's duty is to the client, not the child, and defense attorneys act responsibly when they challenge the testimony of prosecution witnesses.

The Importance of the Present Study

With the highly adversarial nature of the criminal trial in mind, three aspects of the present research are discussed below.

Despite the Stress Caused by Testifying, Society Is Justified in Asking Children to Testify

The U.S. Supreme Court observed that "child abuse is one of the most difficult crimes to detect and prosecute, in large part because there often are no witnesses except the victim" (*Pennsylvania v. Ritchie*, 1987, p. 60). In many cases, the child's testimony is the most vital evidence of wrongdoing. Yet parents and mental health professionals are understandably hesitant to subject children to the rigors of the courtroom.

Testifying is stressful for nearly all witnesses, children and adults alike. Indeed, stress is an *inevitable* by-product of the adversary system. Thus, if children are to continue testifying, the goal of reform efforts cannot be the elimination of stress. Rather, reforms must concentrate on lowering stress and supporting children before and after they testify.

One of the most important findings of the present research is that, although testifying is stressful, children weather the storm. The fact that most children who testify improve with time supports the continued use of their testimony. All child witnesses are entitled to humane and developmentally appropriate treatment at the hands of the legal system, and special accommodations must be made for children at risk of lasting trauma. The overriding theme of this research, however, is that children are strong and resilient. They bounce back. Because children's testimony is indispensable to their protection, the fact that testifying does not appear to cause permanent harm is tremendously reassuring. Provided that steps are taken to support children, judges and prosecutors can feel comfortable asking them to take that long walk from the courtroom door to the witness stand.

Face-to-Face Confrontation with the Defendant Has a Deleterious Effect on Children's Testimony That Justifies Modification of Traditional Methods of Testifying

The present study confirms that many children are anxious about testifying in front of the defendant. The anxiety and fear induced by face-to-face confrontation raise legitimate concerns about the psychological welfare of child witnesses. However, the importance of this study lies, not in confirmation of the universally acknowledged fact that face-to-face confrontation is difficult, but in the finding that, for some children, face-to-face confrontation undermines the completeness of testimony.

The raison d'être of the criminal trial is discovery of truth. Thus, it is vital that testimony be accurate *and* complete. The truth-seeking purpose of the trial is undermined by practices that impair the ability of witnesses to communicate. With the importance of accurate and complete testimony in mind, the most important finding of the present study is that the children who appeared most frightened of the defendant were able to answer fewer of the prosecutor's questions. That is, children who were most intimidated by face-to-face confrontation with the defendant provided *less complete* testimony, undermining the truth-seeking purpose of the trial. The fact that face-to-face confrontation impairs some children's ability to communicate lends resolute and much needed empirical support to reforms that make testifying less stressful.

Testimony via closed-circuit television.—If face-to-face confrontation with the defendant causes anxiety for most children and undermines the ability of some to communicate, the solution appears straightforward: allow children to testify outside the presence of the defendant, and use closed-circuit television to present the child's testimony to the jury. But it is not that simple. The Confrontation Clause of the Sixth Amendment to the U.S. Constitution provides that, "in all criminal prosecutions, the accused shall enjoy the right . . . to be confronted with the witnesses against him." The Confrontation Clause "guarantees the defendant a face-to-face meeting with the witnesses" (*Coy v. Iowa*, 1988, p. 1016).

In *Maryland v. Craig* (1990), the U.S. Supreme Court ruled that the defendant's right to face-to-face confrontation is not absolute and that "a State's interest in the physical and psychological well-being of child abuse victims may be sufficiently important to outweigh, at least in some cases, a defendant's right to face his or her accusers in court" (p. 3167). Thus, the defendant's right to face-to-face confrontation may be curtailed on a showing that confrontation will cause serious emotional distress. Dispensing with face-to-face confrontation is particularly appropriate where confrontation will "impair the child's ability to communicate" (p. 3170). The present study provides valuable support for the argument that face-to-face confrontation impairs the ability of certain children to communicate, thus supporting use of closed-circuit television to allow selected children to testify outside the physical presence of the defendant.

During the past decade, tremendous energy was devoted to passing and defending the constitutionality of laws that allow selected children to testify via closed-circuit television. Such laws are now on the books in a majority of states. Although the present study supports the use of closed-circuit television, it is clear from the Supreme Court's decisions that face-to-face confrontation—although difficult—will remain the norm for child witnesses. Dispensing with confrontation will be the rare exception.

Because closed-circuit television is rarely used, researchers, legislators, judges, and attorneys should redirect their attention elsewhere. The movement in research and practice should be away from "high-tech" solutions and toward readily available, inexpensive, less controversial, and, in the long run, more important methods of helping children cope on the witness stand.

Allowing a supportive adult to accompany the child while the child testi-fies.—Probably the most obvious way to reduce children's stress is to allow a parent or other trusted adult to remain in the courtroom while the child testifies. The present study confirms the emotional importance of a support-ive adult, but the research does more than that. The study reveals that the presence of a supportive adult actually increases children's ability to testify. Presence of a support person increases children's ability to answer questions asked by the prosecutor. Of equal importance, the reassurance afforded by a supportive adult helps children cope with cross-examination by defense counsel. Thus, when a supportive adult is present, children are less likely during cross-examination to recant the identity of the perpetrator, recant central facts, or provide inconsistent answers regarding peripheral issues. These are extremely important findings. The truth-finding function of the criminal trial is measurably enhanced by the simple expedient of allowing a supportive adult to remain in the courtroom. These findings should be used to advocate for expanded use of support persons for child witnesses.

Positioning the child to reduce eye contact with the defendant.—In addition to allowing supportive adults in court, other techniques are available to help children cope with the stress of testifying. Although the Constitution normally mandates face-to-face confrontation, the Constitution does not require witnesses to make eye contact with the defendant (*Coy v. Iowa*, 1988). Thus, children do not have to look at the defendant, and, in appropriate cases, the defendant can be seated outside the child's direct line of sight without affront to the Constitution.

Altering the courtroom to make children more comfortable.—Most criminal courtrooms in the United States are similarly configured and furnished. Does the law permit modification of the solemn halls of justice so that chil-dren can be more comfortable? If modification decreases children's stress and increases their ability to provide accurate and complete testimony, the answer is a resounding yes.

The origins of the contemporary American courtroom are found in England. Historical research discloses that "the courts, as we know them, were developed in the 12th and 13th centuries" (Doerksen, 1990, p. 480). The physical layout of today's courtroom is more the result of practical necessity and convenience than of law or principle. Birks writes that "during the Middle Ages, and even later, courts were rough and noisy places" (Birks, 1972, p. 2). The bar that separates the judge and attorneys from the specta-tors was initially installed to protect the former from the latter. In early times, the king's judges followed the monarch on his travels about the king-dom. Court was held in any convenient location: the great hall of a castle, a meeting room, even an open field. The judge sat on a wooden bench and had no writing desk. As courtrooms became permanent fixtures, and as "law reports began to be printed in the sixteenth century and the practice of examining witnesses in open court was generally adopted, a desk for the judges obviously became desirable" (Birks, 1972, p. 3). Today, of course, the judge's desk is the most prominent feature in the courtroom.

The point of this brief historical sojourn is that the configuration of the modern courtroom is not cast in stone. If altering the furnishings or formalities of the courtroom will make children more comfortable and improve their testimony, nothing in law or the Constitution forbids circumspect modification that does not compromise the seriousness of the proceeding. This is not to say, of course, that judges will rush to change the courtroom. Birks (1972) observes that "there is no doubt that lawyers have always clung to the relics of by-gone days, be they antiquated laws, outmoded dress or ancient ceremonial" (p.1). Encouraging judges to take children's developmental needs into consideration takes time, but the dividends are worth the effort in terms of children's mental health and society's need for accurate decision making.

A Unified Family Court Holds Promise for Reducing the Psychological Trauma of Testifying Multiple Times

The present study and other research indicates that testifying multiple times has a deleterious effect on children. Unfortunately, there is no way to eliminate the likelihood that some children will testify more than once. Not only are children required to testify at various stages of the same legal proceeding, but in some cases there are multiple proceedings in different courts involving the same child, and the child may be required to testify one or more times in each proceeding.

A model that holds promise for reducing the number of times that children testify is a unified family court where all proceedings concerning a child are handled by one court. Versions of the family-court model are in operation in several states (Florida, Hawaii, Missouri, New Jersey, New York, Ohio, Rhode Island, South Carolina, and Vermont). A number of states, including California, Kentucky, Nevada, Virginia, and West Virginia, are experimenting with the unified family court.

Research on Child Witnesses Should Focus Increasingly on Forensically Relevant Information

Research that is relevant to children as witnesses falls into several categories: first, research on children's developmental capabilities, including memory, suggestibility, and moral reasoning; second, research describing background characteristics of cases involving children; third, research on children's performance in actual and simulated forensic contexts.

Developmental Research

Needless to say, most research on child development does not focus on children as witnesses. Nevertheless, much of the basic child development literature has direct forensic relevance. For example, research on children's understanding of the concept of time (e.g., Friedman, 1991) has immediate implications regarding the constitutional principle that the defendant has a right to notice of the charges, including, in some instances, the time frame in which the crime allegedly occurred (Myers, 1992). Basic research on children's memory (e.g., Flin, Boon, Knox, & Bull, in press; Hudson & Fivush, 1991) helps dispel doubts lingering in the minds of some lawyers and judges concerning children's competence to testify. One of the most common methods of attacking the credibility of a witness is to point out discrepancies between the witness's trial testimony and the witness's earlier statements. Research that explains that it is developmentally normal for young children to be inconsistent (e.g., Fivush, 1992; Fivush, Hamond, Harsch, Singer, & Wolf, 1991) goes far toward rehabilitating children's credibility and blunting the sting of cross-examination focused on inconsistencies in the child's description of events.

In the past decade, psychologists turned their attention to developmental research that is increasingly generalizable to actual forensic contexts (e.g., Goodman, Hirschman, Hepps, & Rudy, 1991; Saywitz, Goodman, Nicholas, & Moan, 1991; Saywitz & Nathanson, 1992; Saywitz & Snyder, 1992; Tobey & Goodman, in press; Warren, Hulse-Trotter, & Tubbs, 1991). This research has immensely important implications for the investigation and litigation of child abuse cases. Unfortunately, this valuable research—appearing as it does in the psychological rather than the legal literature—seldom finds its way into the hands of judges and attorneys who could put it to good use in the field. More effective channels are desperately needed to transfer the accumulating psychological knowledge about child witnesses to the legal and judicial professions.

Research Describing Background Characteristics of Cases Where Children Are Involved

Some research on children in the legal system focuses on what may be described as background or demographic features of cases. For example, researchers have studied the percentage of cases accepted for prosecution in a particular jurisdiction, the proportion of children who testify in accepted cases, and the gender, age, socioeconomic status, and ethnicity of children who testify (Education Development Center et al., 1991).

Although background and demographic information about cases is of some interest, such data are of very little practical utility in the day-to-day world of child abuse litigation. Research to date on case characteristics is probably sufficient to explore such matters, and future research on children in the legal system should focus on issues of greater forensic relevance.

Children's Performance in Actual and Simulated Forensic Contexts

In addition to the forensically relevant developmental research described above, the most exciting research on child witnesses is typified by the study described in this *Monograph*. Research focused on improving the accuracy and completeness of children's testimony holds the greatest promise of furthering the welfare of children and the interests of justice (e.g., Saywitz & Nathanson, 1992; Tobey & Goodman, in press).

Directions for Future Research

In 1987 Melton and Thompson observed that "psychologists interested in studying children as witnesses typically have not focused on the most pressing psycholegal issues" (1987, p. 210). Although researchers are increasingly sensitive to the need for greater forensic relevance, vitally important issues remain largely untouched. Psychological research is needed on the topics outlined below.

Children's hearsay statements.—Children disclose abuse to parents, friends, teachers, social workers, therapists, and others. Children's disclosure statements often constitute vitally important evidence of abuse. Nevertheless, disclosure statements are usually hearsay, and the rule in all states is that hearsay cannot be used in court unless the particular hearsay statement meets the requirements of an exception to the rule against hearsay. Thus, in many child abuse cases, it is critically important to determine whether a child's disclosure statement is hearsay and, if so, whether the statement falls within an exception. Although some existing psychological research is relevant to the hearsay rule and its exceptions, there is a great need for psychological research focused directly on the reliability of children's hearsay statements.

Children's inconsistency.—A witness's credibility can be attacked if he or she has given inconsistent versions of critical facts. Psychological research is sorely needed on methods that can be used to maintain children's accuracy while reducing their inconsistency.

Preparing children to testify.—Helping children testify more effectively and at reduced stress is an important goal. At the present time, a wide variety of methods is used to prepare children for testifying. Unfortunately, little research attention has been devoted to preparation techniques, and the efficacy of various methods is open to question. Expanded research attention is necessary (Saywitz & Snyder, 1992).

Interviewing techniques.—The way that children are interviewed by social workers, police officers, attorneys, and others is increasingly important in child abuse litigation. In a growing number of cases, defense attorneys attack the interview methods used with children, arguing that defective interviewing renders children's disclosure statements unreliable. Although much of the research on children's eyewitness testimony is relevant to proper interview technique, much remains to be done, and there is a desperate need for research focused specifically on forensically defensible interview techniques (e.g., Saywitz, Geiselman, & Bornstein, in press).

Lawyers should play an integral role in planning and conducting psychological research on child witnesses.—Few lawyers are schooled in the fine points of psychological research. By the same token, few psychologists have a complete understanding of trial strategy, cross-examination, impeachment, hearsay, and a plethora of other legal issues. Attorneys with experience trying child abuse cases should be involved at every stage of research, from hypothesis to final report. In particular, experienced trial lawyers should be represented on committees that review research proposals.

Conclusion

The research described in this *Monograph* has immediate, far-reaching, and positive implications for child abuse litigation. It forms the benchmark by which to evaluate future research. Measuring up will not be easy.

References

American Bar Association. (1969). *Code of professional responsibility.* Chicago: American Bar Association.
American Bar Association. (1983). *Model rules of professional conduct.* Chicago: American Bar Association.
Birks, M. (1972). Court architecture. In G. R. Winters (Ed.), *Selected readings: Courthouses and courtrooms.* Chicago: American Judicature Society.
Blackstone, W. (1765). *Commentaries on the laws of England.* London.
Coy v. Iowa, 487 U.S. 1012 (1988).
Doerksen, L. E. (1990). Out of the dock and into the bar: An examination of the history and use of the prisoner's dock. *Criminal Law Quarterly,* **32,** 478–502.
Education Development Center, University of North Carolina, and American Prosecutors Research Institute. (1991). *Final report: Child victim as witness research and development program* (Grant No. 87-MC-CX-0026). Washington, DC: Office of Juvenile Justice and Delinquency Prevention, Office of Justice Programs, U.S. Department of Justice.
Fivush, R. (1992). Developmental perspectives on autobiographical recall. In G. S. Goodman & B. L. Bottoms (Eds.), *Understanding and improving children's testimony.* New York: Guilford.
Fivush, R., Hamond, N. R., Harsch, N., Singer, N., & Wolf, A. (1991). Content and consistency in young children's autobiographical recall. *Discourse Processes,* **14,** 373–388.

Flin, R., Boon, J., Knox, A., & Bull, R. (in press). The effect of a five-month delay on children's and adults' eyewitness memory. *British Journal of Psychology*.

Friedman, W. J. (1991). The development of children's memory for the time of past events. *Child Development, 62,* 139–155.

Goodman, G. S., Hirschman, J. E., Hepps, D., & Rudy, L. (1991). Children's memory for stressful events. *Merrill-Palmer Quarterly, 37,* 109–158.

Hudson, J. A., & Fivush, R. (1991). As time goes by: Sixth graders remember a kindergarten experience. *Applied Cognitive Psychology, 5,* 347–360.

Maryland v. Craig, 110 S. Ct. 3157 (1990).

Melton, G. B., & Thompson, R. A. (1987). Getting out of a rut: Detours to less traveled paths in child witness research. In S. J. Ceci, M. P. Toglia, & D. F. Ross (Eds.), *Children's eyewitness memory.* New York: Springer.

Myers, J. E. B. (1992). *Evidence in child abuse and neglect cases.* New York: Wiley.

Pennsylvania v. Ritchie, 480 U.S. 39 (1987).

Saywitz, K. J., Geiselman, R. E., & Bornstein, G. K. (in press). Effects of cognitive interviewing and practice on children's recall performance. *Journal of Applied Psychology*.

Saywitz, K. J., Goodman, G. S., Nicholas, E., & Moan, S. F. (1991). Children's memories of a physical examination involving genital touch: Implications for reports of child sexual abuse. *Journal of Consulting and Clinical Psychology, 59,* 682–691.

Saywitz, K. J., & Nathanson, R. (1992). *Children's testimony and perceived stress in and out of the courtroom.* Manuscript submitted for publication.

Saywitz, K. J., & Snyder, L. (1992). Improving children's testimony with preparation. In G. S. Goodman & B. L. Bottoms (Eds.), *Understanding and improving children's testimony.* New York: Guilford.

Tobey, A. E., & Goodman, G. S. (in press). Children's eyewitness memory: Effects of participation and forensic context. *Child Abuse and Neglect*.

Warren, A., Hulse-Trotter, K., & Tubbs, E. C. (1991). Inducing resistance to suggestibility in children. *Law and Human Behavior, 15,* 273–285.

Wolfram, C. W. (1986). *Modern legal ethics.* St. Paul, MN: West.

CHILDREN AS PARTNERS FOR JUSTICE:
NEXT STEPS FOR DEVELOPMENTALISTS

Gary B. Melton

Several years ago, in an article that Susan Limber and I wrote on psychologists' roles in child maltreatment cases (Melton & Limber, 1989), we suggested that the guiding principle in work with children in such cases ought to be that they are treated as partners in the pursuit of justice. Such a stance, we argued, is a logical corollary of respect for the dignity of children as persons.

At least in some circles, the metaphor of partnership resonated. I understand, for example, that the concept is now highlighted in some continuing education programs for prosecutors.

I am less confident about psychologists' response. Research on child witnesses has burgeoned in recent years (see generally Melton, Goodman, et al., 1992), and it has been influential in public policy (see, e.g., Goodman, Levine, Melton, & Ogden, 1991). Nonetheless, as the field has grown, it has seemed to emulate adult eyewitness research (cf. Saks, 1986) and to give greater and greater attention to less and less important questions that are more and more divorced from central psycholegal issues (Melton & Thompson, 1987; Thompson & Flood, in press).[1] One need not be very cynical

---

[1] Unfortunately, there are signs that child witness research is mimicking the analogous adult field not only in triviality but also in questionable ethics. To respond to objections about external validity of their research, some adult eyewitness researchers (e.g., Hosch, Marchioni, Leippe, & Cooper, 1984) have deceived participants into believing that they were being victimized. Some recent and proposed child witness research has relied on a similar design in which children are led to believe that they are involved in a real police investigation of suspected abuse by their babysitter. To compound the wrong involved in deception and the potential harm that may be evoked by the stress of a police investigation,

to recognize that basic laboratory research on social-cognitive processes in children can be made "relevant" by framing such work as witness research.

The raging controversy on the suggestibility of children (see, e.g., Doris, 1991) is illustrative. There is now no real question that the law (see Melton, 1981) and many developmentalists (see Yarmey & Jones, 1983) were wrong in their assumption that children are highly vulnerable to suggestion, at least in regard to salient details (Melton, Goodman, et al., 1992; see, e.g., Goodman, Aman, & Hirschman, 1987). Although some developmentalists may be challenged to find developmental differences in suggestibility in increasingly arcane circumstances, as a practical matter who really cares whether 3-year-old children are less suggestible about peripheral details in events that they witnessed than are 4-year-old children? Perhaps the question has some significance for developmental theory, but surely it has little or no meaning for policy and practice in child protection and law.

In such a context, I am especially pleased to see Goodman et al.'s work in this *Monograph*. Not only is it by far the most extensive study thus far of actual testimony by children and its effects, but it is also headed in the right direction in regard to choice of topics and variables.

Just as psychologists have been drawn to variables of interest to psychologists in other contexts (e.g., memory, social influence), their consideration (and, for that matter, consideration by many victim advocates) of the effects of testimony has tended to focus on its short-term mental health consequences. That focus is understandable; no one wants to see children upset, and many advocates have started with the assumption that the legal process ought to be seen as traumagenic factor. In the context of the state's compelling interest in the healthy development of children, concern with the level of stress experienced by child witnesses is reasonable.

At the same time, however, one can take as a given that *some* stress is inevitable in the legal process. Adult witnesses who are not nervous before testimony surely are rare. Although induction of anxiety certainly is not in itself a goal of the legal process, it may be an inevitable by-product of fulfillment of goals that the law does have. Legal proceedings have serious consequences, and legal settings must be sufficiently distinctive to symbolize their authority and dignity. Accordingly, both performance anxiety (as a result of the law's concern with the quality of testimony, given the significance of legal decisions, especially in the criminal law) and generalized anxiety (as a result of uncertainty about an unfamiliar setting) are expectable short-term effects of testimony. Demonstration that child witnesses are anxious about testimony thus proves too much. If the law permitted special

---

parents may be asked to join in the deception and to maintain it for weeks. One can only wonder what the effect on children is when they ultimately realize that researchers and parents conspired in lying to them, sometimes across an extended period of time.

procedures whenever witnesses were anxious, its legitimate goals would be frustrated.

Witnesses' anxiety at the time of testimony is relevant to the law if it reaches such a level that it substantially impairs their ability to recount their observations fully and thus impedes the pursuit of justice (cf. Goodman et al., 1991). Insofar, however, as anxiety is being used as a marker of disturbance, long-term effects are much more relevant to the state's interest in children's development than are immediate effects. Accordingly, Goodman et al.'s work in the present *Monograph* is especially useful in its concern with relatively long-term effects on children's adjustment as well as immediate reactions to testimony or the prospect of testimony (when waiting to appear in the courtroom).[2]

Even more to the point, Goodman et al. realized that effects on mental health, whether transient or lasting, are not the only variables of interest; in fact, such variables may not be the most important outcomes for study. Taking for granted that some anxiety is endemic to the legal process, legal authorities may worry more about witnesses' and other participants' perceptions of justice; such a variable is more closely related to the question of whether the legal system is fulfilling its central mission. Such concerns are given special weight by adult research conducted in both the laboratory and the field that shows (*a*) that aggrieved parties often want their day in court, even when the stress engendered by the adversary process is present, and (*b*) that procedural fairness (e.g., having a say) is the principal ingredient in perceptions of justice (Lind & Tyler, 1988). Accordingly, the satisfaction of participants with the legal process may rest less with their level of anxiety associated with the process than with their perceptions of how well the legal system is pursuing justice. Adults, at least, are prepared to endure some stress so that all parties in a dispute can have a say.

For the first time in child witness research, Goodman et al.'s study begins to address such issues. Accordingly, the study focuses not only on mental health concerns but also on a list of perceptions germane to the question of how well the legal system is doing its job: quality of interaction with professionals involved; satisfaction with the case outcome; perception of fairness of the legal system as a whole; and perception of the level of feedback given.

In their choice of variables, Goodman et al. did miss the mark in two ways, however. First, they omitted some of these variables from their inter-

---

[2] I realize, of course, that Goodman et al.'s work does not touch the question of whether effects of testimony on adjustment persist years beyond the event. Nonetheless, the period of time that is covered is sufficiently long that it raises questions about children's marking time developmentally. Hence, it is germane to the state's interest in the socialization of children.

views of children in order to make the questionnaire "more appropriate and less taxing." Goodman et al.'s concern may simply have been with the length of their interview. I suspect, however, that they, like many others in the field, started from the premise that justice concerns are less important to children than to adults (cf. Melton, 1987; Melton & Limber, 1989). Just as prosecutors and caseworkers commonly neglect feedback to child witnesses about the progress of the case (either because the professionals do not regard such information as important to children or because they wish to protect them from the information), Goodman et al. omitted a question on the subject from their interview with children. (The question was included in the closing interviews with the witnesses' parents.)

Second, the questions were worded in such a way that they did not permit a clear assessment of the nature of child victims' perceptions of justice. For example, it is conceivable that the fact that adults' perceptions of justice are affected more by procedure (procedural justice) than by outcome (distributive justice) does not generalize at least to younger children because they may be more focused, relative to adults, on the immediate consequences of legal involvement. Accordingly, children may be more attuned to the verdict and sentence and to their own immediate experience (e.g., anxiety level) in assessing the quality of justice. Laboratory research showing significance, even to 6-year-olds, of procedural justice (Gold, Darley, & Hilton, 1984) and related concepts (see Melton, 1987) pushes, however, toward a hypothesis of generalizability of the adult findings at least to school-age children. So does our recent finding that, regardless of whether children have personal experience in abuse proceedings, the more that they know about the legal process, the more likely that they are to ascribe anxiety to hypothetical victim-witnesses in the courtroom, but also the more likely that they are to describe the process as fair (Melton, Limber, et al., 1992).

Goodman et al.'s questions called, however, only for an overall judgment of the fairness of the legal system (a question that may call more for a political judgment than an assessment of the system's performance in the instant case) and a specific judgment of the desirability of the case outcome. Thus, although Goodman et al.'s study is a good starting point in consideration of the significance of justice concerns for child victims, it does not elucidate the meaning of the court process to them.

Taken as a whole, Goodman et al.'s findings support the Supreme Court's requirement of case-by-case determination of the need for special procedures in child abuse cases. Goodman et al. demonstrate reason for special concern about the well-being of children in the criminal process. In that sense, there is some conflict between the state's interests in protection of child welfare and the pursuit of justice. Goodman et al. also show, however, that testimony is not inevitably traumatic, that some children wish for the opportunity to testify, and that children who do testify generally find the experience not to be as bad as they had feared.

Interestingly, the children who most want to have their day in court are those who are in some of the most negative circumstances (e.g., who have a history of previous abuse; whose caretaker is poorly adjusted) and thus are at high risk for negative effects of testimony. This finding has important policy implications. First, it suggests the need for special procedures in some cases so that children who, in a sense, have the most to tell are able to do so without undue risk. Second, when combined with other findings, it indicates the complexity of determining who is most at risk. Bright-line rules (e.g., age) will not validly discriminate children at high risk of negative effects of testimony. Assessments of overall clinical risk will be overbroad because some children who may be in especially difficult circumstances will benefit from the opportunity to testify. In either instance, assessment of probable effects of *testimony* may not be informative about probable effects of *testimony under special procedures.*

Thus, although Goodman et al.'s work lends credence to the case-by-case approach, it also suggests the difficulty of implementing it. Accordingly, an important next step in research on effects of the legal process is to examine individual differences. Because of the relative rarity of any testimony and the exceptional rarity of testimony under special procedures, such work will necessarily need to be multisite, in order both to have a sufficient number of participants for analyses and to take advantage of natural experiments in legal process.

The risk factors that are identified in the current study are mixed. An overall message is that what happens outside the courtroom probably is more important than what happens inside it. This conclusion is in part a matter of common sense: testimony is relatively rare (with infrequency substantially greater in jurisdictions, unlike the ones studied, in which testimony of children at preliminary hearings is rare), and interaction with the legal system occurs primarily outside the courtroom even when children do testify. It also flows from the data. With the exception of confrontation of the defendant (an aspect of the trial or hearing process that may also disturb adult victim-witnesses), factors mediating the effects of testimony did not include trial procedures or courtroom behavior of the various professionals involved.

This general conclusion may have even greater force in jurisdictions in which more effort is placed on preparation of children for involvement in the legal process. Because few children had even pretestimony tours and some were not even informed why they had come to court, the significance of courtroom procedures could reasonably be assumed to be greater than in jurisdictions where preparation is more systematic.

The most confusing finding of the study is the relation of frequency of testimony to outcome. The meaning of the finding is unclear. The possibility, consistent with other research that Goodman et al. reviewed (Runyan, Everson, Edelsohn, Hunter, & Coulter, 1988), that the finding simply indicates the effects of pendency (i.e., children mark time developmentally when they are literally marking time until their case reaches disposition) seems to be ruled out by other findings about the lack of significance of multiple continuances. Nonetheless, the possibility is left open by the additional finding that children who testify frequently and who appear to be especially negatively affected by the experience are more likely to be exposed to stressors other than the criminal court process. Such children are especially likely to be involved in collateral civil actions (e.g., divorce, removal from home). Thus, although Goodman et al.'s analogue to the effects of multiple physical health stressors on children's mental health may be valid, it is also possible that the effect of frequency of testimony in criminal cases is the product of multiple sources of delay and ambiguity apart from the criminal process itself.[3] If so, reforms oriented toward case consolidation and speedy trials may be important in mitigating adverse effects on child witnesses, regardless of the specific forums involved (e.g., criminal, juvenile, domestic relations). Goodman et al.'s finding about children's aversion to multiple interviews supports that interpretation.

The greatest question about the findings presented in this *Monograph* relates to their generalizability. In a sense, it is a study of three cases (i.e., three courts), and the sample size was insufficient for intercourt comparisons to be made. At least some of the practices in those courts (e.g., frequent testimony at preliminary hearings) are probably atypical of practices in many jurisdictions. At the same time, however, Denver is in many respects the home of child protection, since two major centers on child abuse and neglect and a historic juvenile court are located there, and Colorado statutes give relatively wide discretion for use of special procedures and evidentiary rules in child abuse cases. Accordingly, it is unlikely that modal practice in American courts is much more child sensitive than in the courts that Goodman et al. studied.

Regardless, Goodman et al.'s work is an important first step. The logical next step is to look more carefully at the aspects of legal procedure—both inside and outside the courtroom—that are most likely to support or, conversely, destroy a belief by abused children that they are being treated respectfully and that justice is being done. Examination of that broad question necessarily involves multijurisdictional comparisons, comparisons that

[3] In the same vein, the apparently greater effect of criminal court testimony than has been observed in juvenile court testimony may be related to the fact that criminal child abuse cases are more likely to be accompanied by other legal actions.

also will help answer the question of generalizability of Goodman et al.'s broad findings about the effects of the criminal process on child victims.

References

Doris, J. (Ed.). (1991). *The suggestibility of children's recollections.* Washington, DC: American Psychological Association.

Gold, L., Darley, J. M., & Hilton, J. L. (1984). Children's perceptions of procedural justice. *Child Development, 55,* 1752–1759.

Goodman, G. S., Aman, C., & Hirschman, J. (1987). Child sexual and physical abuse: Children's testimony. In S. J. Ceci, M. P. Toglia, & D. F. Ross (Eds.), *Children's eyewitness memory.* New York: Springer.

Goodman, G. S., Levine, M., Melton, G. B., & Ogden, D. (1991). Child witnesses and the Confrontation Clause: The American Psychological Association brief in *Maryland v. Craig. Law and Human Behavior, 15,* 13–29.

Hosch, H. M., Marchioni, P. M., Leippe, M. R., & Cooper, D. S. (1984). Victimization, self-monitoring, and eyewitness identification. *Journal of Applied Psychology, 69,* 280–288.

Lind, E. A., & Tyler, T. R. (1988). *The social psychology of procedural justice.* New York: Plenum.

Melton, G. B. (1981). Children's competency to testify. *Law and Human Behavior, 5,* 73–85.

Melton, G. B. (1987). Children, politics, and morality: The ethics of child advocacy. *Journal of Clinical Child Psychology, 16,* 357–367.

Melton, G. B., Goodman, G. S., Kalichman, S., Levine, M., Saywitz, K., & Koocher, G. P. (1992). *Empirical research on child maltreatment and the law.* Washington, DC: American Psychological Association, Working Group on Legal Issues Related to Child Abuse and Neglect.

Melton, G. B., & Limber, S. (1989). Psychologists' involvement in cases of child maltreatment: Limits of role and expertise. *American Psychologist, 44,* 1225–1233.

Melton, G. B., Limber, S., Jacobs, J. E., Oberlander, L. B., Berliner, L., & Yamamoto, M. (1992). *Preparing sexually abused children for testimony: Children's perceptions of the legal process* (Final report to the National Center on Child Abuse and Neglect, Grant No. 90-CA-1274). Lincoln: University of Nebraska—Lincoln, Center on Children, Families, and the Law.

Melton, G. B., & Thompson, R. A. (1987). Getting out of a rut: Detours to less traveled paths in child witness research. In S. J. Ceci, M. P. Toglia, & D. F. Ross (Eds.), *Children's eyewitness memory.* New York: Springer.

Runyan, D. K., Everson, M. D., Edelsohn, G. A., Hunter, W. M., & Coulter, D. L. (1988). Impact of legal intervention on sexually abused children. *Journal of Pediatrics, 113,* 647–653.

Saks, M. J. (1986). The law does not live by eyewitness testimony alone. *Law and Human Behavior, 10,* 279–280.

Thompson, R. A., & Flood, M. F. (in press). Getting out of a rut: Little progress yet. *The Advisor* (newsletter of the American Professional Society on Abuse of Children).

Yarmey, A. D., & Jones, H. P. T. (1983). Is the psychology of eyewitness identification largely a matter of common sense? In S. M. A. Lloyd-Bostock & B. R. Clifford (Eds.), *Evaluating witness evidence: Recent psychological research and new perspectives.* Chichester: Wiley.

Gail S. Goodman (Ph.D. 1977, University of California, Los Angeles) is professor of psychology at the University of California, Davis. She was formerly on the faculty of the University of Denver and of the State University of New York at Buffalo. Her research focuses on children's testimony, child abuse, and memory development. Her articles and studies, including the project described in the present *Monograph*, have been cited by the U.S. Supreme Court in decisions regarding child witnesses. She has served as president of the Division on Child, Youth, and Family Services of the American Psychological Association.

Elizabeth Pyle Taub (Ph.D. 1989, University of Denver) is a clinical psychologist and postdoctoral fellow in pediatric psychology at Baylor College of Medicine in Houston. Her research concerns the effects of legal involvement on child victims, gender differences in the emotional effects of child sexual abuse, and children's and families' coping with chronic illness and hospitalization.

David P. H. Jones (D.C.H. 1978, M.R.C. Psych 1980, University of Birmingham) is a psychiatrist at Park Hospital for Children in Oxford, England, and a faculty member at Oxford University. His research on child abuse has focused on interviewing techniques, reports of child abuse to social services agencies, and the emotional effects of criminal court involvement on children. He is associate editor of *Child Abuse and Neglect: The International Journal* and is the former associate director of the C. Henry Kempe Center for the Prevention and Treatment of Child Abuse and Neglect in Denver.

Patricia England (M.S.W. 1989, University of Denver) is a research analyst in the Children's Division of the American Humane Association in Denver. Her research concerns child protective services, including assessment of risk for child abuse, standards and resource management in child protective services, and the operation of central registries.

Linda K. Port (J.D. 1988, University of Denver) is an attorney in Denver. She is affiliated with the law firm of Sherman and Howard and currently specializes in civil litigation.

Leslie Rudy (M.A. Ohio State University) is a doctoral student in clinical psychology. She has conducted research on infant emotional development, child abuse, children's eyewitness testimony, and children's use of anatomically detailed dolls.

Lydia Prado (M.A. 1984, University of Denver) is a clinical psychologist in Los Angeles. Her research concerns background characteristics and attitudes of child sexual abuse offenders.

John E. B. Myers (J.D. 1977, University of Utah College of Law) is professor of law at the University of the Pacific, McGeorge School of Law. He is the author of books and articles on legal issues in child abuse, including *Child Witness Law and Practice* (1987), *Legal Issues in Child Abuse and Neglect Practice* (1992), and *Evidence in Child Abuse and Neglect Cases* (1992).

Gary B. Melton (Ph.D. 1978, Boston University) is Carl Adolph Happold Professor of Psychology and Law at the University of Nebraska—Lincoln, where he also directs the Law/Psychology Program and the Center on Children, Families, and the Law. His research focuses on the relation of children and families to the law. For that work, which has been widely used in the policy arena, he has received the Distinguished Contributions to Psychology in the Public Interest Award from the American Psychological Association (APA), the Harold Hildreth Award from the APA Division of Psychologists in Public Service, the Nicholas Hobbs Award from the APA Division of Child, Youth, and Family Services, and the Donna Stone Award from the National Committee for the Prevention of Child Abuse.

STATEMENT OF EDITORIAL POLICY

The *Monographs* series is intended as an outlet for major reports of developmental research that generate authoritative new findings and use these to foster a fresh and/or better-integrated perspective on some conceptually significant issue or controversy. Submissions from programmatic research projects are particularly welcome; these may consist of individually or group-authored reports of findings from some single large-scale investigation or of a sequence of experiments centering on some particular question. Multiauthored sets of independent studies that center on the same underlying question can also be appropriate; a critical requirement in such instances is that the various authors address common issues and that the contribution arising from the set as a whole be both unique and substantial. In essence, irrespective of how it may be framed, any work that contributes significant data and/or extends developmental thinking will be taken under editorial consideration.

Submissions should contain a minimum of 80 manuscript pages (including tables and references); the upper limit of 150–175 pages is much more flexible (please submit four copies; a copy of every submission and associated correspondence is deposited eventually in the archives of the SRCD). Neither membership in the Society for Research in Child Development nor affiliation with the academic discipline of psychology are relevant; the significance of the work in extending developmental theory and in contributing new empirical information is by far the most crucial consideration. Because the aim of the series is not only to advance knowledge on specialized topics but also to enhance cross-fertilization among disciplines or subfields, it is important that the links between the specific issues under study and larger questions relating to developmental processes emerge as clearly to the general reader as to specialists on the given topic.

Potential authors who may be unsure whether the manuscript they are planning would make an appropriate submission are invited to draft an outline of what they propose and send it to the Editor for assessment.

This mechanism, as well as a more detailed description of all editorial policies, evaluation processes, and format requirements, is given in the "Guidelines for the Preparation of *Monographs* Submissions," which can be obtained by writing to Wanda C. Bronson, Institute of Human Development, 1203 Tolman Hall, University of California, Berkeley, CA 94720.